RATIONAL RITUAL

RATIONAL RITUAL

CULTURE, COORDINATION,
AND COMMON KNOWLEDGE

Michael Suk-Young Chwe

PRINCETON UNIVERSITY PRESS   PRINCETON AND OXFORD

Library of Congress Cataloging-in-Publication Data

Chwe, Michael Suk-Young, 1965–
Rational ritual : culture, coordination, and common knowledge /
Michael Suk-Young Chwe.
p. cm.
Includes bibliographical references and index.
ISBN 0-691-00949-X (alk. paper)
1. Knowledge, Sociology of. 2. Cognition and culture. 3. Collective
behavior. 4. Rites and ceremonies — Social aspects. 5. Rational choice
theory. I. Title.
HM651 .C49 2001
306.4'2 — dc21   00-051683

This book has been composed in Sabon

Printed on acid-free paper. ∞

www.pup.princeton.edu

Printed in the United States of America

10 9 8 7 6 5 4 3 2 1

To Sylvia

Contents

Figures and Tables ⎯⎯⎯⎯⎯⎯⎯⎯

Figures

Tables

Preface

Many people have helped me in many ways. I am grateful for comments received at presentations at the Rational Choice and Beyond: The Future of Political Economy conference at UCLA's Lake Arrowhead; the Interactions-Based Models Workshop in the Social Sciences at the Santa Fe Institute; the Summer Institute for Theoretical Economics at Stanford University; and Cornell University. At New York University, I am grateful for comments received at the Austrian economics workshop and the Department of Politics. At the University of Chicago, I am grateful for comments received at the Applications of Economics workshop; the Chicago Humanities Institute; the Midwest Faculty Seminar on Rationality, Quasi-Rationality, and Rational Choice Theory; John Kelly's graduate anthropology workshop; the Center for the Study of Politics, History, and Culture at Wilder House; and the Department of Political Science. I have also benefited from the suggestions and encouragement of Andy Abbott, Moshe Adler, Penny Becker, Ann Bell, Matthew Benuska, Sam Bowles, Robert Boyd, Randy Calvert, Xiaohong Chen, Karl Chwe, Myron Chwe, John Curran, Jim De-Nardo, Prasenjit Duara, Steve Durlauf, Mahmoud El-Gamal, Jim Fearon, Magnus Fiskesjö, Douglas Gale, Ed Glaeser, Avner Greif, Bernie Grofman, Roger Guesnerie, Anna Harvey, Chang-Ling Huang, John Kelly, Boaz Keysar, Timur Kuran, David Laitin, Namhee Lee, Paula Lee, Susanne Lohmann, Kevin McCabe, Thomas McQuade, Stephen Morris, Ashok Rai, Garey Ramey, Stan Reiter, Peter Rossi, Duncan Simester, Lester Telser, Barry Weingast, Douglas White, Steve Wildman, Pete Wolfe, Libby Wood, and students in my graduate game theory classes. Many of their comments deserve specific attribution, but given the frailties of memory I am not sure that I can do this in a systematic way. Tyler Cowen, Herb Gintis, Sung H. Kim, Rohit Parikh, David Ruccio, Joel

Sobel, and Jim Webster read the first complete draft and
gave very helpful comments. Some material here first appeared in *Rationality and Society* and the *American Journal
of Sociology* (Chwe 1998, 1999b); anonymous referees at
both journals gave very helpful comments. Further comments,
criticisms, and suggestions are welcome at michael@chwe.net
and www.chwe.net.

Norman Bradburn introduced me to Nielsen Media Research, where Ed Schillmoeller and especially Rollie Schmidt
were truly generous. The research assistance of Ben Klemens,
Rob McMillan, and Jeff Newman was essential. I thank
Marshall Hill, the staff and residents of Stateville Correctional Center, and the Illinois Department of Corrections for
their hospitality during our visit to Stateville. Thanks also to
Jim Fearon, Magnus Fiskesjö, Gary Herrigel, and David
Mustard for driving down to Stateville with me. The research here was supported by the National Science Founda-
tion under grant number SBR-9712277. Finally, Peter
Dougherty and Linda Chang of Princeton University Press
were great to work with.

This project was begun at the University of Chicago and
completed after arriving at New York University, and I am
grateful for being able to participate in two of the world's
great intellectual communities. The institution of which I am
most proud to be a member, however, is my family. Throughout my life my mother, Jung-Ja Chwe, has been a model of
strength and faith, and my father, Byoung-Song Chwe, a
model of scholarship and integrity. I continue to learn from
my brothers Karl and Myron and my sister Sylvia. This book
started out of an attempt to understand the books my spouse
Namhee Lee was bringing home, and this is just one of the
many ways in which I appreciate her. We are both grateful
for the support of Namhee's mother, Ki Soon Lee, who
helped us out tremendously at a critical time. Our children
Hanyu and Hana very generously offered some colorful ac-
companying illustrations and demonstrate that joy is possible daily.

RATIONAL RITUAL

1

Introduction

What This Book Is Good For

How do individuals coordinate their actions? Here we consider "coordination problems," in which each person wants to participate in a group action but only if others also participate. For example, each person might want to take part in an antigovernment protest but only if there are enough total protesters to make arrests and police repression unlikely. People most often "solve" coordination problems by communicating with each other. Simply receiving a message, however, is not enough to make an individual participate. Because each individual wants to participate only if others do, each person must also know that others received a message. For that matter, because each person knows that other people need to be confident that others will participate, each person must know that other people know that other people have received a message, and so forth. In other words, knowledge of the message is not enough; what is also required is knowledge of others' knowledge, knowledge of others' knowledge of others' knowledge, and so on—that is, "common knowledge." To understand how people solve coordination problems, we should thus look at social processes that generate common knowledge. The best examples turn out to be "public rituals," such as public ceremonies, rallies, and media events.

Public rituals can thus be understood as social practices that generate common knowledge. For example, public ceremonies help maintain social integration and existing systems of authority; public rallies and demonstrations are also crucial in political and social change. Social integration and political change can both be understood as coordination problems; I am more likely to support an authority or social system, either existing or insurgent, the more others support it. Public rituals, rallies, and ceremonies generate the necessary common knowledge. A public ritual is not just about the transmission of meaning from a central source to each member of an audience; it is also about letting audience members know what other audience members know.

This argument allows specific insights in a wide variety of social phenomena, drawing connections among contexts and scholarly traditions often thought disparate. One explanation of how public ceremonies help sustain a ruler's authority is through their "content," for example, by creating meaningful associations with the sacred. By also considering the "publicity" of public ceremonies — in other words, how they form common knowledge — we gain a new perspective on ritual practices such as royal progresses, revolutionary festivals, and for example the French Revolution's establishment of new units of measurement. It is often argued that public ceremonies generate action through heightened emotion; our argument is based on "cold" rationality.

Ritual language is often patterned and repetitive. In terms of simply conveying meaning, this can be understood as providing redundancy, making it more likely that a message gets through. But it also seems to be important that listeners themselves recognize the patterns and repetition. In terms of common knowledge generation, when a person hears something repeated, not only does she get the message, she knows it is repeated and hence knows that it is more likely that others have heard it. Group dancing in rituals can be understood as allowing individuals to convey meaning to each other through movement. But group dancing is also an excellent common knowledge generator; when dancing, each person knows that everyone else is paying attention, because if a person were not, the pattern of movement would be immediately disrupted.

I then look at examples of people facing each other in circles, as in the kiva, a ritual structure found in prehistoric structures in the southwestern United States, the seating configuration of various U.S. city halls, and revolutionary festivals during the French Revolution. In each of these examples, the circular form was seemingly intended to foster social unity. But how? Our explanation is based on common knowledge generation. An inward-facing circle allows maximum eye contact; each person knows that other people know because each person can visually verify that others are paying attention. I then look at how inward-facing circles specifically, and issues of public and private communication generally, appear in the 1954 feature film *On the Waterfront*.

Buying certain kinds of goods can be a coordination problem; for example, a person might want to see a movie more the more popular it is. To get people to buy these "coordination problem" goods, an advertiser should try to generate common knowledge. Historical examples include the "halitosis" campaign for Listerine. More recently, the Super Bowl has become the best common knowledge generator in the United States recently, and correspondingly, the great majority of advertisements on the Super Bowl are for "coordination problem" goods. Evidence from regular prime-time television commercials suggests that popular shows are able to charge advertisers more per viewer for commercial slots, because popular shows better generate common knowledge (when I see a popular show, I know that many others are also seeing it). Companies that sell "coordination problem" goods tend to advertise on more popular shows and are willing to pay a premium for the common knowledge they generate.

The pattern of friendships among a group of people, its "social network," significantly affects its ability to coordinate. One aspect of a network is to what extent its friendship links are "weak" or "strong." In a weak-link network, the friends of a given person's friends tend not to be that person's friends, whereas in a strong-link network, friends of friends tend to be friends. It seems that strong-link networks should be worse for communication and hence coordinated action, because they are more "involuted" and information travels more slowly in them; however, empirical studies often find that strong links are better for coordination. We can resolve this puzzle by observing that, even though strong links are worse for spreading information, they are better at generating common knowledge; because your friends are more likely to know each other, you are more likely to know what your friends know.

Finally, I consider Jeremy Bentham's "panopticon" prison design, in which cells are arranged in a circle around a central guard tower. Michel Foucault regards the panopticon as a mechanism of power based on surveillance, as opposed to spectacle or ceremony. Foucault and most other observers, however, neglect the fact that Bentham's design includes a central chapel above the guard tower, so that the prisoners can take part in service without having to leave their cells; in other words, the panopticon is to some extent also a ritual structure. The panopticon generates common knowledge in that each prisoner can see that other prisoners are under the same kind of surveillance.

In considering this variety of applications, no attempt is made to treat any single topic, writer, or text comprehensively. The goal instead is to explore unexpected connections, connections that span wide divisions in the social sciences as currently disciplined. Ideas of rationality and culture are often considered as applying to entirely different spheres of human activity and as having their own separate logic. This book argues instead for a broad reciprocal connection. To understand public rituals, one should understand how they generate the common knowledge that the logic of rationality requires. To understand how rational individuals solve coordination problems, one should understand public rituals.

This book draws on scholarly literatures that are subject to ever increasing methodological specialization. I hope that the connections here suggest that an argument can bring together not only diverse subject matter but also diverse methodologies. This book considers, for example, new data (the prices of network television slots, Super Bowl advertising), suggests new explanations for existing empirical regularities (why "strong links" are better than "weak links"), offers new interpretations of aspects of ritual practices (group dancing, repetition, inward-facing circles) and cultural products (the film *On the Waterfront*), and compels a closer reading of classic texts (Bentham's and Foucault's panopticon).

After considering these applications, I briefly consider competing explanations of how rituals affect action, either through direct psychological stimulation or through the emotions that come from being physically together with other people. Next I try to respond to the common objection that common knowledge is not really applicable to the "real world" because people do not actually seem to think through several layers of "I know that he knows that she knows" and so forth.

I then further elaborate on the basic argument. Although one of the main points of this book is that common knowledge generation is an interesting dimension of rituals that can be analytically separated from content, in practice content and common knowledge generation interact in interesting ways; I discuss some examples from marketing and sculpture and the "Daisy" television ad for Lyndon Johnson in 1964. Common knowledge depends not only on me knowing that you receive a message but also on the existence of a shared symbolic system which allows me to know how you understand it.

Because common knowledge generation is important for coordinated action, it is something people fight over; for example, censorship typically cracks down hardest on public communications. Recently political struggles have adopted techniques of modern advertising; for example, in 1993, domestic violence activists successfully pressured the NBC television network for Super Bowl air time. The fact that common knowledge generation is a real resource suggests that "symbolic" resistance should not be underestimated.

Common knowledge is generated not only by communication but also by historical precedent. Political protests and advertising campaigns when trying to generate common knowledge thus draw on history as a resource. Just as history can help create common knowledge, common knowledge can to some extent create history through mass rituals and commemorations. Similarly, common knowledge not only helps a group coordinate but also, to some extent, can create groups, collective identities, "imagined communities" in which, for example, each newspaper reader is aware of millions of fellow readers.

In sum, this book tries to demonstrate three things. First, the concept of common knowledge has broad explanatory power. Second, common knowledge generation is an essential part of what a public ritual "does." Third, the classic dichotomy between rationality and culture should be questioned. This third point is explored more fully in the conclusion. In an appendix, I look at a simple example that illustrates how the argument is made mathematically.

The Argument

In some situations, called "coordination problems," each person wants to participate in a joint action only if others participate also. One way to coordinate is simply to communicate a message, such as "Let's all participate." But because each person will participate only if others do, for the message to be successful, each person must not only know about it, each person must know that each other person knows about it. In fact, each person must know that each other person knows that each other person knows about it, and so on; that is, the message must be "common knowledge."

This truism is a fact of everyday social life and is this book's central argument. It has come up in many different scholarly contexts, from the philosophy of language to game theory to sociology. David Lewis (1969), influenced by Thomas Schelling ([1960] 1980), first made it explicitly; Robert Aumann (1974, 1976) developed the mathematical representation that makes it elementary (see the appendix). It is best expressed in an example.

Say you and I are co-workers who ride the same bus home. Today the bus is completely packed and somehow we get separated. Because you are standing near the front door of the bus and I am near the back door, I catch a glimpse of you only at brief moments. Before we reach our usual stop, I notice a mutual acquaintance, who yells from the sidewalk, "Hey you two! Come join me for a drink!" Joining this acquaintance would be nice, but we care mainly about each other's company. The bus doors open; separated by the crowd, we must decide independently whether to get off.

Say that when our acquaintance yells out, I look for you but cannot find you; I'm not sure whether you notice her or not and thus decide to stay on the bus. How exactly does the communication process fail? There are two possibilities. The first is simply that you do not notice her; maybe you are asleep. The second is that you do in fact notice her. But I stay on the bus because I don't know whether you notice her or not. In this case we both know that our acquaintance yelled but I do not know that you know.

Successful communication sometimes is not simply a matter of whether a given message is received. It also depends on whether people are aware that other people also receive it. In other words, it is not just about people's knowledge of the message; it is also about people knowing that other people know about it, the "metaknowledge" of the message.

Say that when our acquaintance yells, I see you raise your head and look around for me, but I'm not sure if you manage to find me. Even though I know about the yell, and I know that you know since I see you look up, I still decide to stay on the bus because I do not know that you know that I know. So just one "level" of metaknowledge is not enough.

Taking this further, one soon realizes that every level of metaknowledge is necessary: I must know about the yell, you must know, I must know that you know, you must know that I know, I must know that you know that I know, and so on; that is, the yell must be "common knowledge." The term "common knowledge" is used in many ways but here we stick to a precise definition. We say that an event or fact is common knowledge among a group of people if everyone knows it, everyone knows that everyone knows it, everyone knows that everyone knows that everyone knows it, and so on. Two people can create these many levels of metaknowledge simply through eye contact: say that when our acquaintance yells I am looking at you and you are looking at me. Thus I know you know about the yell, you know that I know that you know (you see me looking at you), and so on. If we do manage to make eye contact, we get off the bus; communication is successful.

The key assumption behind this example is that we mainly enjoy each other's company: I want to get off only if you get off and you want to get off only if I get off. For example, say that instead of an acquaintance it is your boyfriend yelling; I care only about your company, but you would rather join him than me. I would thus get off if I knew that you hear the yell, but I need not care if you know that I hear it, because you will get off regardless of whether I do. Situations like the acquaintance example are called "coordination problems": each person wants to act only if others do also. Another term is "assurance game," because no person wants to act alone (Sen 1967). The boyfriend example is not a coordination problem because one person wants to act regardless of whether anyone else does.

In coordination problems, each person cares about what other people do, and hence each person cares about what other people know. Hence successful communication does not simply distribute messages but also lets each person know that other people know, and so on. Two examples illustrate this further.

Rebelling against a regime is a coordination problem: each person is more willing to show up at a demonstration if many others do, perhaps because success is more likely and getting arrested is less likely. Regimes in their censorship thus target public communications such as mass meetings, publications, flags, and even graffiti, by which people not only get a message but know that others get it also (Sluka 1992, Diehl 1992). For nearly thirty years, the price of a loaf of bread in Egypt was held constant; Anwar el-Sadat's attempt in 1977 to raise the price was met with major riots.

Since then, one government tactic has been to make the loaves smaller gradually; another has been to replace quietly a fraction of the wheat flour with cheaper corn flour (Jehl 1996). These tactics are more than just a matter of individual deception: each person could notice that their own loaf was smaller or tasted different but be unsure about how many other people also noticed. Changing the size or taste of the loaves is not the same public event as raising its price.

In January 1984 Apple Computer introduced its new Macintosh computer with a visually stunning sixty-second commercial during the Super Bowl, the most popular regularly scheduled television program each year. The Macintosh was completely incompatible with existing personal computers: Macintosh users could easily exchange data only with other Macintosh users, and if few people bought the Macintosh, there would be little available software. Thus a potential buyer would be more likely to buy if others bought them also; the group of potential Macintosh buyers faced a coordination problem. By airing the commercial during the Super Bowl, Apple did not simply inform each viewer about the Macintosh; Apple also told each viewer that many other viewers were informed about the Macintosh. According to the senior vice president of marketing for Walt Disney Attractions, the Super Bowl "really is the convening of American men, women and children, who gather around the sets to participate in an annual ritual" (Lev 1991; see also Real 1982).

Coordination Problems

I should make clear that a coordination problem is not a "free rider problem," also known as the "prisoners' dilemma." In a free rider problem, no person wants to participate under any circumstances: each person always prefers to "free ride" on the participation of others. We all want to keep the common field green, for example, but everyone has an incentive to let his herd overgraze. "Solving" free rider problems hence requires enlarging people's possible motivations, by for example legal or social sanctions against free riders or repeated contexts in which free riding now might make people not cooperate with you later. "Solving" coordination problems, however, does not require changing peoples' motivations: when everyone cooperates, each person wants to do so because everyone else is. Although the term "collective action problem" is often used to refer only to free rider problems (Olson 1971), some argue that collective actions such as political protest are better described as coordination problems (e.g., Chong 1991; see also Moore 1995). Also, even when solving free rider problems via sanctions, for example, there is the "prior" coordination problem of getting people to participate in a system of sanctions, because usually a person wants to participate in sanctioning only if others do also.

A coordination problem also does not require complete commonality of interest; all that is necessary is that each person's motivation to participate increases (or at least does not decrease) the more others participate. For example, in a political protest, there might be "militants" who want to take part even if only a few others do, "moderates" who want to participate only if many others participate and make it seem a reasonable thing to do, and "hangers-on" who simply want to be part of a big crowd experience and are indifferent about the protest's political aims. As long as for each person "the more the merrier," we have a coordination problem. What is ruled out in a coordination problem is each person not caring what others do, thus making each person's decision completely independent, or each person wanting to participate only if others do not—for example, wanting to go to the beach only when it is not crowded.

In a coordination problem, each person wants to coordinate with others but there can be considerable disagreement about how to coordinate. For example, "many Ghanaians would prefer to rely on a common indigenous national language but differ as to which it should be" (Laitin 1994, p. 626). A given coordination might be very bad for a person, but she still might choose to participate because this undesirable coordination is better than the even worse possibility of nonparticipation. For simplicity, we generally assume that the only issue is whether to participate; the issue of how people fight over how to coordinate is considered later.

Common Knowledge

Here I offer some examples to illustrate how common knowledge is a useful everyday concept, part of the commonsense meaning of "public," and also how common knowledge can to some degree be distinguished from "content" or "meaning."

A recent development in U.S. political campaigning is "push-polling," in which voters are asked leading questions in some impartial guise. As part of a contract with Bob Dole during the 1996 Republican presidential primary, Campaign Tel Ltd. employees identifying themselves with "Iowa Farm Families" made more than ten thousand telephone calls to Iowa voters attacking opponent Steve Forbes's flat tax plan. In response to criticism, a Dole campaign spokesperson defended the tactic, saying that the calls "amounted to messages that have mirrored our television commercials" (Simpson 1996). Regardless of whether the "messages" were the same, the crucial distinction is that the telephone calls were not common knowledge: each person who received a call had little idea of whether or how many other people were similarly called. A television commercial, on the other hand, is common knowledge at least to some degree because a person seeing a television commercial knows that other people are seeing the same commercial. This distinction holds even though a "mass audience" of at least ten thousand people received telephone calls, and would remain even if fewer than ten thousand people saw television commercials.

The New York Metropolitan Opera finally decided in 1995 to display translations of the libretto during performances. However, instead of "supertitles," in which translations are projected on a screen above the stage, the Met developed its own "Met Titles," in which each member of the audience has her own small electronic screen, which she can turn on or off. According to one reviewer, " 'Met Titles' are markedly superior to the systems of most theatres: . . . they don't become part of the performance's public discourse" (Griffiths 1995). Even if most people turned their screens on, the translations would not be common knowledge because a person reading them does not know if other people are reading (or will admit to reading) them.

For users of electronic mail, common knowledge is nicely described as the difference between cc: ("carbon copy") and bcc: ("blind carbon copy"). When one sends a message to several people at the same time via the To: address line or via carbon copy, each receiver gets the list of people to whom the message is sent. With blind carbon copy, however, each receiver gets a message such as "recipient list suppressed." In terms of the transmission of messages from one person to another, carbon copy and blind carbon copy are the same; they differ in whether they allow recipients knowledge of other recipients. Because carbon copy allows each recipient to have the email addresses of other recipients, it invites bulk email "spamming." But this disadvantage is sometimes outweighed by the need to generate common knowledge. For example, "Ms. Tadaki said having her e-mail list borrowed made her rethink how she addresses messages to a large list. 'Next time I send out a change of address, I will definitely do Bcc,' she said. Even so, Ms. Tadaki said there were still cases when she would use the To field for group messages — namely, an invitation to a party or some other social gathering. 'It allows people to see who else is coming or who is invited' " (Stellin 2000).

Common knowledge is affected not only by technology, but also by how people choose to communicate. Brian McNaught (1993, p. 53) tells of an accountant friend who says "I'm sure my boss knows I'm gay . . . but I'm also sure he doesn't want to talk about it and doesn't want me to talk about it." Here her boss knows that she is a lesbian, and she knows that he knows, but she cannot talk about it with him, because then he would know that she knows that he knows. The accountant and her lover hosted a pretheater cocktail party for "the accounting firm's employees and their spouses. . . . Once the boss and his wife finally arrived, all the employees quickly headed out the door with their dates. Joining them was the lesbian accountant who took the arm of her male escort. Her lesbian lover stayed home. . . . In this case, everyone knows that there is a homosexual present but pretends that it isn't so." If the accountant went with her lover instead, people would know that everyone else knows; the fact that she is a lesbian would become public, common knowledge.

Common knowledge is in some sense the opposite of a secret. George describes how he came out as a gay man: "I told Peter first . . . then I told Fred . . . and told them not to tell anyone else or talk about it with anyone else until I did. . . . After I talked with other people in our circles, then they did, so after a while everyone was talking with everyone else about it instead of having this big secret that everyone bottled up inside" (Signorile 1995, p. 76). Initially, George told other people individually; even though everyone knew that George was gay, for each person it was still a secret. Once Peter and Fred initiated conversation, people began to know that other people knew; the secret evaporated only after common knowledge was formed.

Common knowledge is not always desirable; sometimes people deliberately avoid it. A male hotel butler who intrudes upon a naked female guest, instead of acting embarrassed and thereby letting the guest know that he knows, might say loudly, "Pardon me, sir." Dissimulation can prevent common knowledge (Kuran 1995), but, as the examples here illustrate, honesty alone is not sufficient.

Most interpretations of cultural practices focus on the "content" or "meaning" of what is communicated. Much of the point of this book is that cultural practices must also be understood in terms of "publicity" or, more precisely, common knowledge generation. This distinction, which cannot

be rigidly maintained (as discussed later), still is useful. To
see the distinction, consider two examples. Abner Cohen
(1974, p. 133) describes the Friday midday prayer in Islam
as both "a demonstration of allegiance to the existing political order . . . [and] an ideal strategic occasion . . . for staging
rebellion . . . in the presence of all the men of the community
in one gathering." The public execution, described by Michel
Foucault (1979, pp. 50, 58–60) as a "ritual of armed law,"
was actually quite unstable: "the people, drawn to the spectacle intended to terrorize it, could express its rejection of
the punitive power and sometimes revolt. Preventing an execution that was regarded as unjust, snatching a condemned
man from the hands of the executioner, obtaining his pardon
by force . . . overturned the ritual of the public execution."
An event's meaning can be "overturned," but the aspect of
common knowledge, necessary for both mass legitimation
and mass rebellion, remains constant.

Where the Argument Comes From

Without attempting a comprehensive survey, it is worth noting at least that the concepts here are basic enough to have
come up in several different contexts. Lewis (1969, p. 6)
finds the idea of coordination problem in David Hume's example of several people in a rowboat, each rower wanting to
row at the same rate as all the others. The notion of common knowledge arises immediately when thinking about language (Clark and Marshall 1992, Schiffer 1972); knowledge
of the knowledge of others and so on is necessary even for
basic conversation. For example, to respond affirmatively to
my friend's question, "Do you want some coffee?" I would
say, "Coffee would keep me awake" only if I know that my
friend knows that I want to study rather than sleep (Sperber
and Wilson 1986). Coordination problems and how they are
solved were considered early on by Schelling ([1960] 1980),
and common knowledge was modeled mathematically by
Aumann (1976); these issues have been pursued in game the-

ory (for a survey, see Geanakoplos 1992), as well as logic, theoretical computer science, and philosophy (e.g., Gilboa 1998). "Higher-order beliefs" (beliefs about the beliefs of others) and the distinction between public and private announcements are increasingly relevant concepts for economics and finance (e.g., Chwe 1999a, Morris and Shin 1999, Shin 1996). Common knowledge relies on people having a "theory of mind," an ability to understand the mental states of other people; how exactly the theory of mind works and develops is an important question for cognitive neuroscience (e.g., Baron-Cohen, Tager-Flusberg, and Cohen 2000). In the popular literature, common knowledge comes up periodically in recreational mathematics and logic puzzles (e.g., Stewart 1998).

Social psychologists developed the concept of "pluralistic ignorance," which refers to a situation in which people hold very incorrect beliefs about the beliefs of others, and is in this sense the absence of common knowledge. To take one of many examples, in a 1972 survey 15 percent of white Americans favored racial segregation, but 72 percent believed that a majority of the whites in their area favored segregation (O'Gorman 1979; see also Shamir 1993). Most see pluralistic ignorance as a distortion at the individual level (e.g., Mullen and Hu 1988; see O'Gorman 1986): a person reduces dissonance by thinking that her own view is the majority view, for example. Recently it has been applied to the Soviet Union and eastern European states, the idea being that dissatisfaction was widespread but that few people knew how widespread it was. These accounts focus on limited communication: criminal penalties for self-expression, a government-controlled press, and a lack of social ties. "The reduction of pluralistic ignorance," due to modern communication technology and increased foreign contacts, "led . . . to a political wave of tremendous power" (Coser 1990, p. 182; see also Kuran 1991) and the collapse of these regimes.

In his analysis of law, Niklas Luhmann (1985, pp. 26–28) emphasizes the *double contingency* of the social world": not only is the physical world uncertain, but the actions of other people are uncertain. Understanding "the perspectives of others . . . is only possible if I see others as another I . . . [who] is as free to vary his behaviour as I am." Hence there is a need, which social institutions help fill, to stabilize "*expectations of expectations.* . . . Moreover, it needs to be considered that there is a third, fourth, etc. level of reflexivity, namely expectations of expectations of expectations and expectations of expectations of expectations of expectations, etc." According to Luhmann, "the reciprocity of perspectives and the constituted meaning of the you for the I can be traced back to German idealism."

2

Applications

Ceremonies and Authority

How do cultural practices such as rituals and ceremonies constitute power? Clifford Geertz (1983, p. 124) writes that "the easy distinction between the trappings of rule and its substance becomes less sharp, even less real; what counts is the manner in which . . . they are transformed into each other." Lynn Hunt (1984, p. 54) is more direct: during the French Revolution, "political symbols and rituals were not metaphors of power; they were the means and ends of power itself." How exactly does this happen? What is the mechanism?

Our explanation starts by saying that submittting to a social or political authority is a coordination problem: each person is more willing to support an authority the more others support it. For example, Jürgen Habermas interprets Hannah Arendt as saying that "the fundamental phenomenon of power is not the instrumentalization of *another's* will, but the formation of a *common* will in a communication directed to reaching agreement" (Habermas [1977] 1986, p. 76; see also Postema 1982 and Weingast 1997). This coordination problem can result not only from a desire to reach consensus but also from intimidation: according to Michael Polanyi (1958, p. 224), "if in a group of men each believes that all the others will obey the commands of a person claiming to be their common superior, all will obey this person as their superior. . . . [A]ll are forced to obey by the mere supposition of the others' continued obedience." Because submitting to an authority is a coordination problem, an authority creates ceremonies and rituals that form common knowledge.

Geertz's explanation starts with a society's core cultural beliefs, its "master fiction"; a symbolic communication such as a ceremony or ritual is powerful through an "intimate involvement" with this master fiction. Geertz (1983) illustrates this in three examples of royal progresses. In sixteenth-century England, a progress was didactic and allegorical: "four townsmen [were] dressed to represent the four virtues — Pure Religion, Love of Subjects, Wisdom, and Justice," with Elizabeth Tudor representing the Protestant virtues of "Chastity, Wisdom, Peace, Perfect Beauty, and Pure Religion." In fourteenth-century Java, which had a hierarchical, nested-circle world view, the king Hayam Wuruk appeared in the middle of the procession, with each of the four compass points represented by a princess. In eighteenth- and nineteenth-century Morocco, a core belief was that "one genuinely possesses only what one has the ability to defend," and hence "as long as he could keep moving, chastening an opponent here, advancing an ally there, the king could make believable his claim to a sovereignty conferred by God." For our purposes, the more basic question is not how these three cases differ but how they are the same: that is, why progresses? "Royal progresses . . . locate the society's center and affirm its connection with transcendent things by stamping a territory with ritual signs of dominance. . . . When kings journey around the countryside . . . they mark it, like some wolf or tiger spreading his scent through his territory, as almost physically part of them."

But this interpretation misses, or takes for granted, the most obvious aspect of progresses — their very large audiences, "crowds of astonished peasants" (Geertz 1983, p. 132); under this interpretation, the audience would be powerfully affected regardless of how large or small it is. Our interpretation focuses exactly on publicity, the common knowledge that ceremonies create, with each onlooker seeing that everyone else is looking too. Progresses are mainly a technical means of increasing the total audience, because only so many people can stand in one place; common knowledge is extended because each onlooker knows that others in the path of the progress have seen or will see the same thing. That the monarch moves is hence not crucial; mass pilgrimages or receiving lines, in which the audience moves instead, form common knowledge also. Under our interpretation, widespread ritual signs of dominance do not by their omnipresence evoke transcendence but are rather more like saturation advertising: when I see the extent of a vast advertising campaign, I know that other people must see the advertisements too. This is quite different from the wolf analogy, if taken seriously: a lone animal knows to stay away from another's area by smelling the scent at a given place; no one perceives or infers the entire scent trail (for that matter, scents keep away rivals, whereas progresses are for "domestic" consumption).

Another way to say this is to consider how Geertz uses the term "public," as in the following: "anything that somehow or another signifies is intersubjective, thus public, thus accessible to overt and corrigible *plein air* explication" (Geertz 1980, p. 135). Geertz is making the methodological point that culture is not about "unobservable mental stuff" but about "socially established structures of meaning" by which people communicate and are therefore available for analysis and understanding (Geertz 1980, p. 135; 1973, p. 12). But the use of "public" to include anything intersubjective is much broader than common usage, as in, for example, "public apology" or "public tribunal." My income tax returns are intersubjective and to some extent accessible, but they are not public. In an extended discussion, Geertz (1973, p. 6) notes that the meaning of a wink cannot be reduced to the physical act of twitching one's eye, but depends, among other things, on the understanding between two people that the wink is done "conspiratorially," "without cognizance of the rest of the company." In other words, the meaning of a wink depends on it not being common knowledge. This, of course, makes sense; however, it is not clear that something purposefully conspiratorial should be placed under the category of "public." Using "public" so broadly makes it difficult to explore the dimension of publicity — or, more precisely, common knowledge generation — in cultural practices; it does not allow us to see that the whole point of some ceremonies is to make public. According to Geertz (1980, p. 135), "arguments, melodies, formulas, maps, and pictures are not idealities to be stared at but texts to be read; so are rituals, palaces, technologies, and social formations." Speaking glibly, rituals and ceremonies are not just "texts" but also publishing processes (see also Keesing 1987).

Geertz's explanation focuses on the meaning or content of progresses, while ours focuses on publicity, how progresses create common knowledge. The point is not that content and meaning are unimportant, but that the aspect of publicity, common knowledge generation, must also be considered.

Lynn Hunt (1984, p. 88), in her analysis of the symbolic and cultural practices of the French Revolution, writes that "radicals . . . exposed to themselves and everyone who watched the fictionality of the Old Regime's 'master fiction.' . . . a new political authority required a new 'master fiction.' . . . the members of society could invent culture and politics for themselves." In adopting Geertz's framework, Hunt shows its weakness: if cultural practices can be used to create a new master fiction, their power cannot be based solely on association with the existing master fiction. But Hunt (1984, p. 54) continues: "Governing cannot take place without stories, signs, and symbols that convey and reaffirm the legitimacy of governing in thousands of unspoken ways. In a sense, legitimacy is the general agreement on signs and symbols. When a revolutionary movement challenges the legitimacy of traditional government, it must necessarily challenge the traditional trappings of rule as well. Then it must go about inventing new political symbols that will express accurately the ideals and principles of the new order."

Here Hunt acknowledges that it is not enough simply to invent new symbols or systems of meaning; they must also be made to enjoy "general agreement." Although what this means is not made explicit, by using the term "unspoken," perhaps Hunt means common knowledge, something each person knows and can take for granted that everyone else knows. Indeed most of the practices Hunt examines, especially revolutionary festivals, an "incurable mania for oaths" (Jean-François La Harpe, quoted in Hunt 1984, p. 21), and even planting liberty trees and wearing revolutionary colors, are ceremonies that generate common knowledge, in which each participant can readily see that others are participating.

Revolutionaries also established new units of weight and measure (the metric system) and invented a new calendar, with new holidays and the seven-day week replaced by a ten-day "decade." That most of the world today drives on the right is also due to the French Revolution: the previous custom in western Europe was to drive on the left, but because ordinary people walked on the right to face the oncoming traffic, that direction was considered more democratic (Young 1996). Hunt (1984, p. 71) interprets these changes in terms of propaganda, so that "even clocks could bear witness to the Revolution," but we can be more specific. Getting people to accept new conventions of trade, time, and travel is a co-ordination problem, less important than but similar, in terms of its mass scale, to the coordination problem of getting people to accept a new government. By successfully solving one coordination problem, revolutionaries build the common knowledge helpful in solving the second: a person might not know the extent to which other people support a new regime but would know that others consented at least to using its new weights and measures. William Sewell (1985, p. 77) understands the revolution's new units of measure and time in terms of its ideology: revolutionaries wanted to transform people's "experiences of space and time. . . . Their revolution recognized a new metaphysical order; wherever existing social practices were based on the old metaphysics they had to be reconstituted in new rational and natural terms." But changing weights, measures, and the calendar is particularly effective not simply because they change the way that a given individual thinks about the revolution or the physical world, but because they change how individuals interact with each other; they change what an individual knows about other individuals.

James Scott (1990, pp. 203–4, 56) distinguishes explicitly between public communications, the "public transcript," and nonpublic communications, the "hidden transcript": for example, "the Catholic hierarchy . . . understands that if large numbers of their adherents have chosen to live together out of wedlock, such a choice . . . is of less institutional significance than if these same adherents openly repudiated the sacrament of marriage." Similarly, "if the sharecropping tenants of a large landowner are restive over higher rents, he would rather see them individually and perhaps make concessions than to have a public confrontation." Again, the question is why.

Scott (1990, pp. 41, 224) sometimes claims that the emotions that "breaking the silence" brings about have causal significance. For example, immediately after the live radio broadcast of black boxer Jack Johnson's victory over the white Jim Jeffries in 1910, "there were racial fights in every state in the South and much of the North. . . . [I]n the flush of their jubilation, blacks became momentarily bolder in gesture, speech, and carriage. . . . Intoxication comes in many forms." A public declaration creates "political electricity"; to understand how widespread the impact of a public declaration is, "we can metaphorically think of those with comparable hidden transcripts in a society as forming part of a single power grid. Small differences in hidden transcript within a grid might be considered analogous to electrical resistance causing loss of current."

But Scott's main explanation is the same as ours, that public declarations create common knowledge: *It is only when this hidden transcript is openly declared that subordinates can fully recognize the full extent to which their claims, their dreams, their anger is shared by other subordinates.* When Ricardo Lagos accused General Pinochet of torture and assassination on live national television, he said "more or less what thousands of Chilean citizens had been thinking and saying in safer circumstances for fifteen years"; the openness and publicity, not the content, of his speech, made it a "political shock wave." "In a curious way something that everyone knows at some level has only a shadowy existence until that moment when it steps boldly onto the stage" (Scott 1990, pp. 223, 207, 215–216).

Even so, Scott (1990, p. 48) does not realize the power of his main explanation. "Imagine, for example, a highly strati-fied agrarian society in which landlords *recently* had the co-ercive force to reliably discover and punish any tenants or laborers who defied them. . . . So long as they maintained a bold ritual front, brandishing their weapons, celebrating past episodes of repression, maintaining a stern and determined air . . . they might exert an intimidating influence all out of proportion to the elite's actual, contemporary power." Here Scott, like Geertz, bases the power of state rituals on associa-tion: for Scott an association with previous weapons-based power, for Geertz an association with the master fiction. But as Scott (1990, p. 49) notes, "the successful communication of power and authority is freighted with consequences inso-far as it contributes to something like a self-fulfilling proph-ecy. If subordinates believe their superior to be powerful, the impression will help him impose himself and, in turn, con-tribute to his actual power." Hence the publicity of rituals, their "successful communication," can constitute power all by itself; association is helpful but not absolutely necessary. Instead of resistances in a power grid, one could say that differences in hidden transcripts cause weaknesses in com-mon knowledge. For example, this is how Mika Gupta de-scribes her feelings reading Simone de Beauvoir's *The Second Sex* as a young woman in Calcutta: "Her words had a po-tency because she knew how *I* felt. . . . At the same time I found her alienating. . . . There were no spaces into which I could fit my experience as a 'bastard of cultures'" (Okely 1986, p. 4). Finally, one need not explain the reaction to Jack Johnson's live radio victory in terms of "intoxication": if I allow myself one moment to behave authentically, it might be rational to do so when I think that others will also.

How Do Rituals Work?

An often-quoted example from Rousseau ([1755] 1984) is the "stag hunt," in which each person can either join with others and hunt for a stag, or hunt for a rabbit by himself. If everyone hunts for a stag together, they succeed, and everyone gets more than one rabbit's worth of food. But if only a few people hunt for the stag, they surely fail, and each would be better off just getting a rabbit. Hence each person will hunt for the stag only if others do also. One could spread the message "Let's hunt for the stag at sunrise tomorrow" sequentially by word of mouth, but a more effective way to communicate would be to get everyone together in a meeting, so that not only would everyone know about the plan, but everyone would also immediately see that everyone else knows about the plan, forming common knowledge. If one calls this meeting a "ritual," then according to our argument, the purpose of a ritual is to form the common knowledge necessary for solving a coordination problem.

As argued earlier, coordination problems include not only quite specific tasks such as group hunting but also overarching matters such as political and social authority. Earlier we considered authority simply in terms of each person's decision about whether to consent to a given regime, but authority generally includes much more, such as systems of social status, implicit and explicit rules of behavior, and the entire set of ideas and institutions that guide social interaction. A ritual should then make public, make common knowledge, in this case not a specific hunting plan, but a set of beliefs and rules. There is some support for this idea in Victor Turner's analysis of the rituals of the Ndembu of Zambia: "ritual is a periodic restatement of the terms in which men of a particular culture must interact if there is to be any kind of a coherent social life. . . . There is no doubt that Ndembu, by their religious activities, call public attention to axioms of conduct" (Turner 1968, pp. 6, 269).

Due to internal pressures (conflict between the Ndembu principles that a man should live with his maternal relatives but also has a right to make his wife live with him in his own village), external pressures (an encroaching Western money economy), and the personal petty conflicts that unavoidably arise, there is a constant need to "shore up" rules of behavior through rituals. In fact some rituals "seem almost 'designed' to contain or redress [social strains and tensions] once they have begun to impair seriously the orderly functioning of group life" (Turner 1968, p. 280). More generally, "in many African tribes rituals are performed most frequently when a small community is in danger of splitting up" (Turner 1968, p. 278). If recognizing and obeying rules of behavior is a coordination problem, then if tensions and hostilities threaten these rules, "remedial" actions are immediately required, because the more people who "opt out" of the system, the less incentive everyone else has to remain.

How exactly do rituals help in social integration? Turner (1969, p. 179) quotes at length the words of an Ashanti high priest (recorded and translated by Rattray 1923): "Our forbears . . . ordained a time, once every year, where every man and woman, free man and slave, should have freedom to speak out just what was in their head, to tell their neighbors just what they thought of them, and of their actions, and not only to their neighbours, but also the king or chief. When a man has spoken freely thus, he will feel his *sunsum* [soul] cool and quieted, and the *sunsum* of the other person against whom he has now openly spoken will be quieted also. . . . [W]hen you are allowed to say before his face what you think you both benefit." Turner interprets this in terms of a need for periodic "levelling" of status in which "the high must submit to being humbled." Under our explanation, what is important is being able to speak openly and publicly, to another's face, making what was previously furtive, personal, a grudge you hold that others might only suspect, common knowledge and hence publicly resolvable.

To understand how a ritual does what it does, it is usually thought necessary to understand the varied meanings of the symbols and words used. But several people have pointed out the need to understand aspects of ritual that cannot easily be understood in terms of "meaning"; for example, words spoken in rituals typically involve lots of repetition, and are structured, in rhyme, verse, or song, for example, in "canonical parallelism" (Jakobson 1966). Maurice Bloch (1974, p. 56) takes as an example the circumcision ceremony of the Merina of Madagascar, noting that "the participants use their language in a particular way: formalised speech and singing. A purely formal analysis of the symbols of the ceremony would simply miss out this central fact." Frits Staal (1989, p. 264) notes that "the Sanskrit that occurs in mantras is often used in an unintelligible fashion. . . . Even those mantras that say something or have meaning are not used like linguistic utterances when they are ritually used." Staal locates the ritualness of mantras not in the meaning of the words but in the patterns and rhythms of their spoken syllables.

Repetition of the same phrase can be understood as providing redundancy, in the spirit of information theory. But as Stanley Tambiah (1985, p. 138) notes, information theory is not directly applicable because rituals are more about "interpersonal orchestration and . . . social integration and continuity" than transmitting information. According to Tambiah, one must think of "'meaning,' defined not in terms of 'information' but in terms of *pattern recognition.*" Interpreted in terms of common knowledge generation, repetition is about not just making sure that each person gets a message but also making sure that each person can recognize the repetition and thus know that everyone else gets the message. Claude Lévi-Strauss (1963, p. 229) asks "why [are] myths, and more generally oral literature, so much addicted to duplication, triplication, or quadruplication of the same sequence? . . . [T]he answer is obvious: The function of repetition is to render the structure of the myth apparent." In our interpretation, the function of repetition is to render repetition apparent.

Bloch argues that the reason that language is formalized in ritual (a "fixity of sequencing of speech acts") is to limit severely the possible set of meanings that can be conveyed: "the formalisation of speech therefore dramatically restricts what can be said so the speech acts are either all alike or all of a kind and thus if this mode of communication is adopted there is hardly any *choice* of what can be said. . . . An utterance instead of being potentially followed by an infinity of others can be followed by only a few or possibly only one" (Bloch 1974, pp. 62–63). This formalization is for Bloch (1974, pp. 64, 71) the source of ritual authority: "it is because the formalisation of language is a way whereby one speaker can coerce the response of another that it can be seen as a form of social control. . . . *You cannot argue with a song*." In our interpretation, each participant in a ritual can never be completely sure that the other participants are paying full attention. Formalization, the fact that once one phrase is said, the next automatically follows, assures each participant that even a person who momentarily loses attention or mentally drifts off for a while can still easily figure out what other people must have heard. With lots of repetition and structure, a person who is only paying attention at the end can still know what a person who only paid attention at the beginning heard. On a longer time scale, performing rituals the same way year after year gives a young person confidence that he hears what older people heard years ago, and an old person confidence that future people will know what he knows. The certainty of the ritual sequence generates authority not by enforcing responses but by helping generate common knowledge.

Bloch also includes under formalization "partial vocabulary" and "illustrations only from certain limited sources, e.g. scriptures, proverbs" (Bloch 1974, p. 60). Both of these aspects of ritual also help form common knowledge; it is mutually evident to all that the vocabulary and illustrations used are commonplace and cannot possibly be the source of any confusion. Tambiah (1985, p. 128) finds that rituals use "multiple media by which the participants experience the event intensely"; hence a person in a ritual has a strong presumption that other people are experiencing the same thing, if not via one medium then through another. Similarly, Turner (1968, pp. 21, 269) notes that although a ritual includes "rich multivocal (or 'polysemous') symbolism," it is "a dramatic unity. It is in this sense a kind of work of art." In other words, a ritual employs several parallel ways of saying the same thing, and thus each person knows that even if another person might not "get it" in one way, she can in another. Audience participation — for example, call and response — helps create common knowledge: each person can see from the gestures or speech of others that they are in fact paying attention. Tambiah (1985, p. 123) quotes A. R. Radcliffe-Brown's interpretation of dance as enabling "a number of persons to join in the same actions and perform them as a body." Although one can say that "bodily movements are a kind of language and that symbolic signals are communicated through a variety of movements from one person to another" (Bloch 1974, p. 72), our interpretation is somewhat simpler: group dancing "as a body" is an ideal way of creating common knowledge because if any person loses interest, this becomes immediately evident to everyone because the pattern of movement is disrupted.

Inward-Facing Circles

One specific way to generate common knowledge, as mentioned in our bus example earlier, is eye contact. For larger groups the closest thing to eye contact is for everyone to face each other in a circle, which enables each person to see that everyone else is paying attention. Perhaps this is one reason why inward-facing circles help in coordination.

A common feature of prehistoric structures throughout what is now the southwestern United States is the kiva. Built partially underground, kivas were typically circular, and people presumably sat facing each other; some kivas had a masonry bench built along the wall (Figure 1). The large "great kivas" of Pueblo Bonito in Chaco Canyon, New Mexico, for example, had impressive features such as deposits of beads in niches in the walls. The difficulty of their construction suggests their importance: "in a limited sense Great Kivas can be considered public monumental building" (Lekson 1984, p. 52; see also Lipe and Hegmon 1989). Most interpreters see the function of kivas, especially the large great kivas, as ritual structures for the village, where public activities could

Figure 1. Kiva, Chetro Ketl, Chaco Canyon, New Mexico.

be held. Their purpose was to integrate the village across household and family groups, which presumably involves solving coordination problems.

In his survey of city halls in the United States and Canada, Charles Goodsell (1988, p. 158) finds that curving seating rows feel friendlier than the more traditional parallel linear rows: they "help to create the impression that the occupants are bound together." In Fort Worth's city hall, the seats are arranged in coincentric inward-facing circles (Figure 2); the architect Edward Durrell Stone hoped "that a council meeting would be in the vein of a town hall meeting. . . . [I]n the circle, members of the audience would have visual contact with each other as well as the council, therefore enabling them to observe feelings and responses" (Goodsell 1988, p. 166). Note that Goodsell's explanation of the effect of circular seating is based on content, an interpretation of its meaning; Stone's explanation is based on common knowledge, the ability of people to see each other.

Mona Ozouf ([1976] 1988, pp. 130–31) finds that for revolutionary festivals in the French Revolution, circular forms

Figure 2. City Hall, Fort Worth, Texas.

were considered ideal (Figure 3): there was an "obsession
with the amphitheater . . . which enabled the spectators to
share their emotions equally and to see one another in perfect reciprocity." Another reason was that organizers wanted
to emphasize inclusivity by making the boundary of the festival as loose as possible; a circle is nicely enclosed by the
outermost spectators, and can grow organically as more
spectators arrive. Finally, the "circle was an emblem of national unanimity."

Again, the last reason relies on content, the symbolic
meaning of a circle, whereas the first relies on common
knowledge, people being able to see each other. Ozouf's quotations ([1976] 1988, pp. 308, 131) from contemporary observers set up this distinction nicely: according to Mouille-
farine fils, "the circle is more symbolic of the facts to be
immortalized, its solidity deriving from reunion and unani-
mous accord"; De Wailly writes that "the audience placed in
front of the boxes thus becomes a superb spectacle, in which
each of the spectators seen by all the others contributes to

Figure 3. Festival of Liberty, October 1792.

the pleasure that he shares." Is the circle symbol or communication technology?

Ozouf ([1976] 1988, p. 136) answers directly: "What was
most important in the conversion of churches into *temples
décadaires* was not the ingenuity employed in transforming a
former Eternal Father into Father Time . . . or a Saint Cecelia into a goddess of Equality. . . . The essence of such con-
versions was to be found in those abolished side chapels,
those truncated transepts, that re-creation within the church—
by means of flags, hangings, foliage—of a place that could
be taken in at a glance." It's not just a matter of changing
symbols, but of changing the physicality of ceremonial
spaces to make it difficult for someone to see you without
you also seeing them, better to generate common knowledge.

On the Waterfront

Perhaps one reason why an inward-facing circle symbolizes
solidarity is because it generates common knowledge, just as
one reason that a ceremonial sword symbolizes power is because it is similar to an actual weapon. Here I illustrate how

the inward-facing circle is used very specifically in *On the Waterfront*, a 1954 feature film directed by Elia Kazan and written by Budd Schulberg, which tells a story of how disparate longshoremen gradually come together to fight against a gang of corrupt union "officials." The unity of the corrupt gang is emphasized by their circular huddle (Figure 4).

The longshoremen's passivity and powerlessness are also emphasized spatially: they appear outdoors and exposed, never in a place of their own. When Father Barry, the local priest, attempts to hold a meeting in the basement of his church, the workers sit scattered all over the pews, avoiding eye contact and not saying anything; the meeting is soon broken up anyhow by gang members with clubs. As they flee, Father Barry convinces Kayo Dugan to testify to the crime commission currently investigating the corrupt union (earlier Joey Doyle was killed because he testified). With the first serious eye contact between a worker and anyone else,

Figure 4. "Payday." From *On the Waterfront*.

Father Barry promises: "You stand up and I'll stand up with you."

But as Dugan loads whisky boxes in a ship's hold, a load of boxes "accidentally" falls on him. Father Barry's eulogy exhorts the workers to stand up for themselves, and this is the turning point in the film. When Dugan's body is placed on a pallet in the ship's hold, the scene is typical of how the workers are portrayed: it is a chaotic, unfocused mess, with boxes and broken glass scattered all over and people looking in several different directions (Figure 5).

It soon becomes clear, however, that this is the first time that the worker public experiences something, the funeral ritual, together; it is the first time that the workers have common knowledge of something. Father Barry and Pop Doyle accompany Dugan's body as the crane pulls them upward, and the setting is much like the Greek amphitheater, with rising concentric rings of spectator participants (Figure 6).

Figure 5. About to ascend. From *On the Waterfront*.

Figure 6. Ship's hold as amphitheater. From *On the Waterfront*.

Because one of its messages is that "ratting" on former
friends can be heroic, *On the Waterfront* is obviously related
to Kazan's willing testimony to the House Un-American Affairs Committee (see, e.g., Biskind 1975). But communication, public and private, powerful and impaired, is not just a
"subtext" but is actually a recurrent theme. Throughout,
there is the constant punctuation of the ships' horns and
steam whistles, reminding us of the power of the employers,
their ability to communicate publicly. When Terry tells Edie
Doyle, Joey's sister, that he was unwittingly involved in
Joey's murder, Edie responds by first covering her ears with
her hands, then by covering her eyes, and finally by covering
her mouth. After *Waterfront*, Kazan and Schulberg continued their inquiry into publicity by making *A Face in the
Crowd* in 1957, in which an Arkansas wandering drunk was
discovered by a reporter, given his own radio and then television show, and thereby became a national demagogue.

Believe the Hype

Although advertising's overall social significance is often acknowledged, it is not at all clear exactly how it works. David W. Stewart (1992, p. 4) notes that "it is curious and a bit embarrassing that more than ninety years of advertising research still leaves open the question of advertising effectiveness. . . . What is not well understood are . . . the conditions under which advertising will have effects and the specific form of those effects." Michael Schudson (1995, p. 22) explains that "what must astonish people with casual beliefs in the vast power of the media is how difficult it is to measure media influence. . . . '[W]e really don't know a great deal' [says one media consultant]. 'If we knew more we would be dangerous.'" Here I argue that advertising can be partly understood in terms of common knowledge generation.

Buying a particular good might be a coordination problem for various reasons. Technological reasons include "network externalities" (Katz and Shapiro 1994): a person would be more likely to buy a Macintosh computer, fax machine, or DVD player if others buy it also, because a person's utility from buying it increases as the number of other people buying it increases. "When you go to Office Depot to buy a fax machine, you are not just buying a US$200 box. You are purchasing for $200 the entire network of all other fax machines" (Kelly 1997). Social reasons can be also quite strong: I might want to see the movie *Titanic* simply because I want to be able to talk about it with my friends and co-workers. I might be more likely to buy Miller Lite beer if it is popular, so that when friends come over, I can give them beer which I expect they will like. Coordination problems might exist for newly introduced goods, because of the fun or distinction in being part of a new popular trend, or simply because one doesn't feel as foolish when purchasing a new good if one knows that others are buying it too. "Pleasure from a good is greater when many people want to consume it, because a person does not want to be out of step with what is popular" (Becker 1991, p. 1110).

Several people have suggested that the mass media not only distribute messages to receivers but also let each receiver know about other receivers. James G. Webster and Patricia F. Phalen (1997, p. 120) write that "it is likely that people watching a media event know that a vast audience is in attendance. Such awareness is part of the event's appeal, and the media are generally eager to report the estimated worldwide audience." Diana Mutz (1998) studies how the mass media affect people's opinions of the opinions of others (see also Davison 1983 on the "third-person effect"). Naomi Wolf (1991, pp. 74, 76) finds that women's magazines "bring out of the closet women's lust for chat across the barriers of potential jealousy and prejudgement. What are other women really thinking, feeling, experiencing. . . . All can participate in this one way in a worldwide women's culture." To understand how the mass media generate common knowledge, we should look at advertising campaigns for products that need it the most, namely "coordination problem" goods.

One wildly successful campaign that helped inaugurate the modern advertising era in the 1920s was the "halitosis" campaign for Listerine. Originally sold as a surgical antiseptic, Listerine was remarketed as a mouthwash; "halitosis," a previously obscure medical term for bad breath, enabled Lambert Pharmaceutical to "refer to bad breath without quite so much offense" (Lambert 1956, p. 98). The extent of the advertising was immense, at its height reaching a combined magazine and newspaper readership of 110 million per month (Vinikas 1992, p. 33), and profits increased fortyfold in seven years (Marchand 1985, p. 18). To explain its success, it is easy to refer to the "hygienic spirit of the decade" (Sivulka 1998, p. 158), but this was more likely effect than cause; the campaign has been credited as singlehandedly "making the morning mouth-wash as important as the morning shower or the morning shave" (Lennen 1926, p. 25). It was also one of the first campaigns to deploy "advertising dramas," depicting for example a forlorn young woman who unknowingly had bad breath and was therefore "Often a bridesmaid but never a bride." But the campaign's success was due not only to effective communication from advertiser to each individual consumer but also common knowledge creation: communication, however implicit, among consumers.

"Halitosis" was not just a polite but also a medical term: the ad copy made clear that halitosis was the "medical term meaning offensive breath." It thus allowed a person to think of herself not as an individual slob but as the victim of a condition commonly shared, just as more recently people suffering from chronic fatigue syndrome seek its recognition as a "real" disease, and a member of Overeaters Anonymous acknowledges that "having the name 'compulsive overeating' on it helps. It reminds me that I am not alone; this is a problem other people have too" (Chapkis 1986, p. 25). Using Listerine as a mouthwash was not something an individual person would be likely to try all by himself: "You would have been considered vile had you swirled it around your mouth at the turn of the century. It should be used on the walls of operating rooms" (Twitchell 1996, p. 144). A person would be more likely to try Listerine as a mouthwash if he knew that others were trying it also; it thus helped to have each potential consumer think that there was an entire subpopulation with the same affliction and who thus might try the same cure.

By observing the campaign's vast scale alone, each person could surmise that others were seeing the ads also. But on top of this, the advertising theme also was consistently centered around the issue of (the lack of) common knowledge. The victim of halitosis never knew that other people knew about her bad breath: lead lines included "If your friends were entirely frank with you" (Figure 7), "They say it behind your back," "Ask your best friend if you dare!" and "He wouldn't have done it knowingly" (*Literary Digest*, November 21, 1921, p. 45; December 17, 1921, p. 54; February 11, 1922, p. 59; December 9, 1922, p. 58; see also Marchand 1985, p. 18). Since friends in polite society could not talk about it openly and explicitly, the only way to communicate about it, and thereby make sure that one's hygiene met social

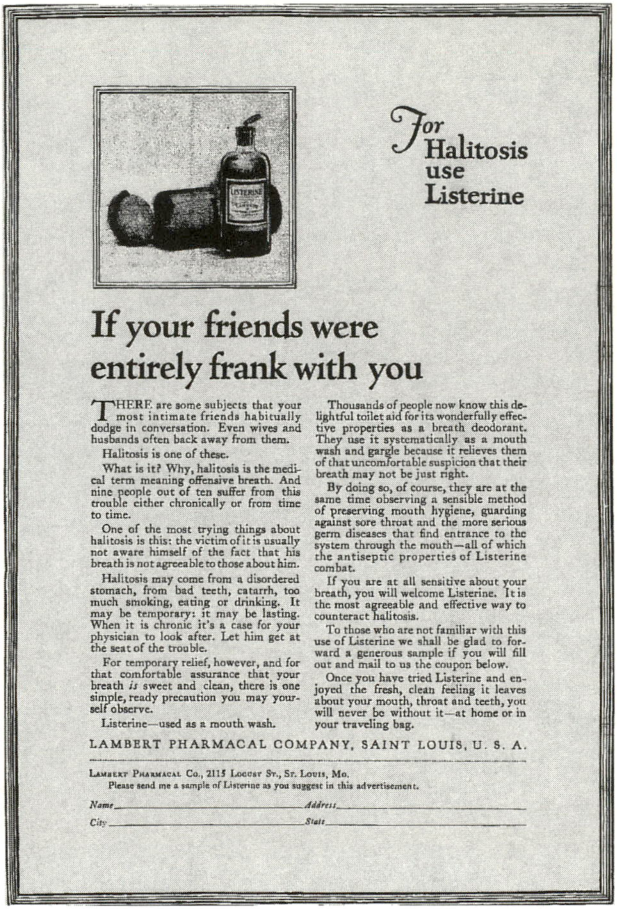

Figure 7. "If your friends were entirely frank with you."
Literary Digest, November 21, 1921.

standards, was implicitly through advertising. Once the
premise of incomplete metaknowledge was established, these
ads "stepped forward to fill one of the many vacuums of
adequate communication and advice" (Marchand 1985, p.
22). The campaign for Kotex, also in the 1920s, faced the
same problem: it was not something one could easily talk

about (because women found it embarrassing to ask for by name, it was sold on counters where women could pick up the plain brown packages and leave their money anonymously [Sivulka 1998, p. 163]). Women were thus assured by advertisements saying that Kotex was something "Which 8 in 10 Better-Class Women Have Adopted" (Marchand 1985, p. 23).

The halitosis campaign should not be considered an artifact of a more delicate, less media-savvy era. Figure 8 shows baseball fans at Cleveland's Jacobs Field who look up to see an airplane pulling a banner advertising anonymous HIV testing. Obviously the irony here is the airing of such a sensitive issue as AIDS publicly and even festively on a bright sunny day at the ballpark. AIDS is the disease of our era, but the tactic is all halitosis: I would be more likely to get an HIV test if I knew that doing so was not unusual, but I wouldn't find this out through everyday conversation; at the ballpark, looking up at the plane, however, it is obvious to all that everyone is seeing the same thing.

Many have argued that advertising "creates needs" that people would not have cared about otherwise; for example, in the early 1900s "the visible application of cosmetics was deemed highly inappropriate by middle-class Americans" (Vinikas 1992, p. 57). But perhaps it is less a matter of creating individual isolated needs than of tapping into the deep and basic need of each individual to conform to community standards, an ever present coordination problem. Thus a mechanism for generating common knowledge, such as national magazine advertising, would have greatest advantage in matters over which existing common knowledge mechanisms, such as conversation among friends, are weakest: "delicate" and "taboo" issues such as personal hygiene and appearance. People fighting the external influence of modern advertising would thus try to reduce its advantage by generating common knowledge internally, "breaking the taboo" and speaking freely among themselves. Thus, for example, a book in which twenty-five women do nothing more than speak openly about their own bodies, looks, and self-image

Figure 8. "True Story: A Sign of the Times." Jacobs Field, Cleveland, Ohio. By derf, 1996.

can be understood in terms of political mobilization: "there can be no truly empowering conclusions until our beauty secrets are shared" (Chapkis 1986, p. 3).

Some goods create their own demand in some sense by definition; for example, although people do have a general demand for entertainment, demand for a particular movie often does not exist until it is released. If a person wants to see what is popular, if only because she wants to know what everyone else is talking about, seeing a movie is a coordination problem. To take one example, "'Independence Day' is a mega metaphenomenon — a pseudo event in which the audience prides itself on being part of the hype" (Wolcott 1996). One of the first movie and theater publicists was Harry Reichenbach, who got his start literally traveling with the circus and later launched stars such as Douglas Fairbanks and Rudolph Valentino. Reichenbach was a common knowledge virtuoso. When a rival theater, the Lyric, threatened his client S. Z. Poli's Bridgeport monopoly, Reichenbach responded first with a whispering campaign, spreading rumors that the Lyric was built unsafely on quicksand; of course, if this allegation had been made publicly, it could have been denied publicly. Next, after he learned that the Lyric planned to open with the two plays "Divorçons" and "Under Southern Skies," he placed a half-page ad in the local newspaper in which Poli thanked "those few people who had asked him to revive 'Divorçons' and 'Under Southern Skies' that season, but both plays had been given so long and so often in Bridgeport that half the town knew the cues and for that reason he would not play them" (Reichenbach 1931, p. 130). Of course, no one had seen either play before, but this ad made everyone think that everyone else had. Five years before Carl Sandburg's (1936, p. 8) image of the moon as billboard ("Daddy, what's the moon supposed to advertise?"), Reichenbach turned the Manhattan sky green for the premiere of a Clara Kimball Young picture (Reichenbach 1931, p. 164).

Hollywood since the 1970s has seen the increasing dominance of the "high concept" film, intended to have a huge audience immediately upon release (Wyatt 1994). It used to be that movies would routinely open in New York City and be gradually released across the country. But that changed in the 1970s. After the film *Billy Jack* opened poorly in a traditional release, it reopened in May 1973 in southern California "with an unheard of one-week ad expenditure of $250,000. . . . The response was phenomenal: the first week's gross of $1,029,000 represented the largest boxoffice take in Southern California film history" (Wyatt 1994, pp. 110–11). This marketing technique, known as "four-walling," was widely imitated; now movie ads routinely include their nationwide opening dates, presumably hoping that people will come on that very day (but see also De Vany and Walls 1999).

This trend has had implications far outside the movie industry; the Macintosh "1984" commercial was apparently inspired by the marketing of the film *Star Wars* (Johnson 1994). Now mammoth marketing efforts routinely try to take advantage of "synergy": to take an early example, the premiere of *King Kong* in 1976 was accompanied with the introduction of "Jim Beam *King Kong* Commemorative bottles . . . *King Kong* sportswear . . . 7-Eleven *King Kong* cups, *King Kong* peanut butter cups, and *King Kong* GAF Viewmaster slides" (Wyatt 1994, p. 150). Personifying this trend is the basketball player Shaquille O'Neal, who throughout his product endorsements (including Reebok, Spalding, and Pepsi), video games, books, rap recordings, and movie roles presents the same consistent image, the same trademarked name "Shaq," and even the same "Shaq" logo. Michael Jordan, representing an earlier marketing era, presents a different image in each of his product endorsements (Lane 1993).

More recently Reichenbach's hucksterism has been revived by the computer industry. On August 24, 1995, Microsoft lit up the Empire State Building in red, blue, orange, and green lights to introduce its Windows 95 operating system. In an unprecedented worldwide marketing effort totaling an estimated $1 billion in advertising expenses (Auerbach and Crosariol 1995), Microsoft bought the entire press run of the

London *Times* and distributed it free with an advertising supplement, placed a six-hundred-foot Windows 95 banner on the CN Tower in Toronto, the world's tallest free-standing structure, towed a four-story-high Windows 95 box into Sydney Harbor, and hand-delivered the first copy in the Philippines to President Fidel Ramos. The hype was necessary because, as one industry analyst observed, "it would be a self-fulfilling prophecy if few decide to upgrade" (Helm 1995). In other words, people upgrade only if they think that others will too; upgrading is a coordination problem. According to Microsoft chairman Bill Gates, "you have to create a lot of excitement to overcome inertia" (Helm 1995). For coordination problem goods such as computer operating systems, you need more than just excitement: you need common knowledge.

The best common knowledge generator in the United States is the Super Bowl, the most popular program on network television that occurs regularly. Ever since the Macintosh's introduction at the Super Bowl in 1984, it has been the premier showcase for the introduction of new products: the Discover card was introduced on no fewer than six commercials during the 1986 Super Bowl (Horovitz 1987), and products such as Chrysler's Neon automobile, various Nike and Reebok new athletic shoe models, and, less successfully, Crystal Pepsi have all made their debut there (Lev 1991, Johnson 1994). The Discover card is a nice example of a "network externality": consumers use them only if enough retailers accept them, and retailers accept them only if enough consumers use them. People might be more likely to buy a new model of car if they know that many other people will buy it: an unpopular car might be more difficult or expensive to service, for example. Purchasing goods like cars, clothing, shoes, beer, and soft drinks, which to some degree are consumed publicly, can be a coordination problem if people want to show that they are participating in what's popular.

If we look at goods advertised on the Super Bowl (Table 1, compiled from *USA Today* stories) we see the preponderance

TABLE 1
Products Advertised on the Super Bowl, 1989–2000

Category	Number of Commercials	Typical Advertisers and Products
Beer	86	Budweiser, Bud Light
Soft drinks	71	Pepsi, Diet Coke
Cars	70	Dodge, Toyota, Nissan
Communications	49	FedEx, AT&T, Nokia
Movies	39	*Independence Day*
Clothing and shoes	37	Nike, Reebok
Financial services	33	Visa, American Express
Fast food	20	McDonalds
Household medications	20	Advil, Tylenol
Web sites	20	Monster.com
Snack foods	20	Doritos
Computers	13	Intel, Apple Computer
Shaving products	10	Gillette
Locks	8	Master Lock
Consumer electronics	6	Panasonic
Food	6	Pork, Hormel Chili
Tires	6	Goodyear, Michelin
Airlines	4	Delta Airlines
Cruise lines	4	Norwegian Cruise Lines
Hotels	3	Holiday Inn
Retail stores	3	Sears, Just For Feet
Batteries	2	Rayovac
Car rental	2	Alamo, Hertz
Cereals	2	General Mills, Kellogg
Exercise machines	2	Soloflex
Motor oil	2	Quaker State
Public service	2	U.S. Census
Shampoos	2	Selsun Blue
Vacuum cleaners	2	Dirt Devil
Video rentals	2	Blockbuster Video
Building materials	1	Owens Corning
Deodorants	1	Faberge Power Stick
Eyeglasses	1	Luxotica
Motorcycles	1	Yamaha

of "social" goods like cars, beer, soft drinks, movies, clothing, and shoes, whose purchase might be understood in terms of a coordination problem, and the relative absence of "nonsocial" goods like batteries, motor oil, and breakfast cereal. The preponderance of beer, cars, and shaving products might be explained in terms of a demographic slant toward men; however, most of the soft drink ads, say for Diet Pepsi, and ads for financial services, such as American Express, are not particularly male-oriented. Also notable is the preponderance of classic "network economy" companies such as Federal Express, AT&T, and Visa, which do not seem to have an obvious connection, in terms of demographics or product association, with the Super Bowl.

The most recent trend in Super Bowl advertising is the appearance of ads for web sites. In the 1999 Super Bowl, there were just three commercials for web sites: Hotjobs.com spent half of its yearly revenues on a single spot and Monster.com bought two slots (McGraw 1999). In the 2000 Super Bowl, however, thirteen more web sites joined in. Hotjobs.com and Monster.com are both job listings sites, and their growth is a coordination problem in a very pure sense: a person wants to look for a job at Monster.com only if she knows that possible employers are also looking there, and vice versa. That Monster.com's advertising strategy is about common knowledge and not about the Super Bowl's "prestige" or demographic targeting is suggested by its buying of air time also on the Barbara Walters interview of Monica Lewinsky, a much-hyped television event with viewership approaching Super Bowl levels. The trade publication *Adweek* observed: "Maybe it doesn't mean anything, but we were struck by the number of Internet companies that decided to advertise on last Wednesday's exclusive Barbara Walters interview with Monica Lewinsky, as other advertisers allegedly stayed away. . . . Call it the Super Bowl of scandal" (Taylor 1999).

If the Super Bowl's huge audience is not obvious enough, some Super Bowl commercials include it as a theme: "Bud Bowl" ads pit one kind of Budweiser beer against another in a "stadium" of 16,000 Bud can spectators (Kahn 1989); in a spot for Rold Gold pretzels, Jason Alexander seemingly parachute-lands on the Super Bowl field during the game, to the surprise of the sportscasters and the wild cheers of the crowd ("Super TV Ad Jumps into Homes" 1995). The Super Bowl as premiere venue is even used as metaphor. The Super Bowl takes place on "Super Sunday" each year; hence print ads for the launching of Paramount's UPN television network with the premiere of the series *Star Trek: Voyager* proclaimed "Before Super Sunday, Get Ready for Super Monday! We're launching a new television network and a new starship to boldly take you where no one has gone before" (*Chicago Reader,* January 13, 1995). The association is not with football but common knowledge creation, which makes sense if each person is more likely to watch if he thinks that his friends will.

Ever since cable television and even more so with the internet, network television overall has been in decline. "A contemporary television blockbuster like *Seinfeld* draws only one-third the audience, as a percentage of the total, that saw 1960s network hits like *The Beverly Hillbillies*" (Rothenberg 1998), back in the days when a large, furniture-like television set served as a home's "electronic hearth" (Tichi 1991). Media events like the Super Bowl (more generally see Dayan and Katz 1992) are television's last stronghold: regardless of increasing fragmentation, there remain the "communal pleasures of watching a popular show at the same time as everyone else in the country. 'The shared experience is the value of television,' . . . asserts CBS president [Howard] Stringer" (Zoglin 1993). Even spokespersons for the "new media" recognize the importance of common knowledge. With the internet, a person can easily tailor her own daily newspaper to include only those stories relating to her own interests. However, David Weinberger (1995), who heads a web marketing company, notes that "such micro-customization would strip newspapers and other documents of one of their primary strengths: helping bestow a sense of community on a group. . . . The fact that the document I'm looking at is the same for all who receive it . . . establishes a baseline of expectations about what we, as a community, are all supposed to know."

George W. S. Trow (1997, pp. 88, 36) writes that the "most important moment in the history of television was the moment when a man named Richard Dawson, the 'host' of a program called *Family Feud,* asked contestants to guess what a poll of a hundred people had guessed would be the height of the average American woman." Trow goes on to complain that there is "no *reality* whatsoever. No *fact* anywhere in sight. . . . I would like to know in what way the producers of this show *aren't* culpable." But is television's main purpose to transmit facts? If *Family Feud* is the most important program in the history of television, it is because it rewards people for knowing what others know.

The Price of Publicity

Television advertising provides not only interesting anecdotes, but also quantitative evidence. Here I look at 119 brands advertised on three U.S. networks (ABC, CBS, and NBC) during three months representative of a network year (October 1988, February 1989, and July 1989; the data set is available from the author). By seeing on which shows a given brand advertises, and finding demographic and cost data available on each show, it is possible to get an idea of that brand's overall advertising strategy.

I call a good "social" if a person is more likely to buy it the more other people buy it; buying a social good is a coordination problem. If we assume that viewers generally know which shows are popular, we can say that when a product is advertised on a popular show, not only do many people see the ad, each viewer knows that many other people see the ad. Hence our argument would say that social goods should be advertised on popular shows. The data here suggest that social goods are in fact advertised on more popular shows and also that advertisers of social goods are willing to pay more per viewer to do so.

The audience size ("ratings") and demographics of virtually every network television program are estimated by Nielsen Media Research. Nielsen also estimates the cost of commercial slots on a given program, based on reports from the television networks, not on actual transactions. Actually a slot on a given program usually does not have "its own" price; slots are often bought and sold in blocks in a complicated sequence of negotiations (Poltrack 1983). These cost data, the only such available (with the exception of actual contracts made available to the Federal Communications Commission in 1980; see Fournier and Martin 1983), at least are relied upon by the advertisers and television networks themselves. Information on which brands advertise on which programs is the greatest limitation of our data set: only those brands which Nielsen clients contract for are available, and only for the months October, February, and July (for a description, see Webster and Lichty 1991, p. 222). This quite limited sample of 119 brands is neither random or representative, but at least for each brand we know the complete television advertising strategy, in full cost and demographic detail, during three months chosen by Nielsen to represent a television season.

Table 2 shows the social and nonsocial brands by product type; very crudely, along with computers, I include in "social" brands those which are typically consumed with people outside the household: in our sample, the social brands are the Apple Macintosh, IBM hardware, the U.S. Army, Dominos Pizza, Gallo Wines, and thirteen brands of beer. Computers are social goods because of technological compatibility. The idea with beer (and wine and pizza similarly) is that I might prefer to buy a beer brand which I think my guests know and like, I might not want to be the only person who brings a strange brand of beer to a party, or I want to participate in the collective experience of drinking the same kind of beer as everyone else (see also Pastine and Pastine 1999a, 1999b). This classification is fairly ad hoc, but at least we might say that goods that are typically consumed inside the household are less likely to be social goods because no one can see what others are consuming. According to Gary Becker (1991, p. 1110), "a consumer's demand for some goods depends on the demands by other consumers. . . . [R]estaurant eating, watching a game or play, attending a concert, or talking about books are all social activities in which people consume a product or service together and partly in public."

Table 2 also shows the average audience size and average cost per thousand for each product type. What these terms mean can be explained in an example: if Brand X pays $25,000 for one thirty-second slot on a show with an audience of 9 million households and pays $10,000 each for two thirty-second slots on a show with an audience of 3 million households, the average audience size for Brand X is 5 million and the average cost per thousand is $3, since the total cost is $45,000 and there are a total of 15 million "gross impressions" (see Webster and Lichty 1991, p. 192). Average audience size indicates the popularity of the shows that a brand's commercials appear on, and average cost per thousand indicates how expensive those commercials are. Audiences are measured here in terms of households, and during this time there were 90.4 million households in the United States.

The first thing to notice is that average cost per thousand is consistently higher for the social brands than for the nonsocial brands (exceptions are shaving and cameras and film processing). In other words, beer and pizza advertisers are willing to spend more per household than battery and deodorant advertisers. If a beer advertiser pursued the same advertising strategy as a deodorant advertiser, he could get roughly twice as many total impressions for the same amount of money. Second, audience sizes for social brands are larger than for nonsocial brands. With two exceptions (bath and soap, and shaving) nonsocial categories have audience sizes of less than 7 million, and with two exceptions (armed forces and computers) social categories have audience

TABLE 2
Average Audience Size and Average Cost per Thousand for Various Brand Categories

Category	Number of Brands in Category	Typical Brand in Category	Average Audience Size (millions)	Average Cost per Thousand (dollars)
Social brands				
Armed forces	1	U.S. Army	5.9	10.1
Beer	13	Coors Light	7.3	10.5
Computers	2	Apple Macintosh	5.4	9.5
Pizza	1	Dominos Pizza	9.5	9.1
Wine	1	Gallo Wines	7.9	9.1
Total	18		7.1	10.2
Nonsocial brands				
Baby care	2	Chubs Baby Wipes	4.6	4.8
Bath and soap	3	Caress Beauty Bar	7.4	7.0

Nonsocial brands (cont.)

Batteries	Energizer	2	5.3	5.8
Bleach and detergent	Clorox Bleach	6	5.9	4.6
Cameras and film processing	Canon Cameras	2	6.9	10.7
Candy	Carefree Gum	2	6.1	4.2
Cereal	Kellogg Crispix	27	6.0	6.3
Deodorant	Arrid Deodorant	6	5.6	5.2
Food	Shedds Spread	12	5.5	5.0
Hair care	Head & Shoulders	10	5.5	5.0
Household cleaners	Lysol	14	5.3	3.9
Household medications	Nuprin	10	5.3	5.2
Pet food	Milk Bone Biscuits	1	5.7	4.8
Shaving	Atra Plus Razor	2	7.8	9.7
Toothpaste	Aquafresh	1	4.3	5.5
Wood finishing	Minwax	1	4.5	5.1
Total		101	5.6	5.4

sizes of greater than 7 million. If we exclude computers, Canon cameras, and the U.S. Army because they are the only brands in the sample that have a price of more than a few dollars, the distinction is clearer.

We graph average audience size and cost per thousand for all 119 brands in Figure 9. Again, the first finding is that social brands tend to be advertised on popular shows. The second finding is that campaigns for social brands pay a higher cost per viewer.

These findings support our argument, but of course there are competing explanations. The first and most obvious is that audiences of popular shows have more favorable demographic characteristics. Nielsen reports on more than forty demographic categories, including age, sex, region, county size, rural versus urban, household size, presence of children, household income, and cable television subscription. Because we know demographic characteristics for each show, and we know which shows an advertiser places commercials on, we can determine the demographic composition of the audience of a brand's complete campaign.

A second possible explanation has to do with a campaign's cumulative effect over a month. There is the issue of "au-

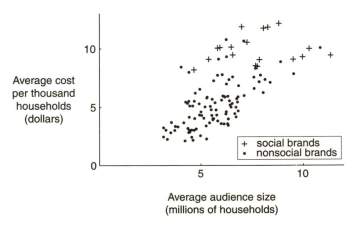

Figure 9. Cost per thousand versus average audience size.

dience duplication": two commercials that each reach 5 million people might together reach fewer than 10 million people because their audiences to some degree overlap. A commercial slot on a program that reaches 10 million people all at once might thus cost more even though it provides the same total number of exposures. Fortunately, data are available on each campaign's "four-week reach," the percentage of households that saw at least one commercial during the month, and we use this as our measure of cumulative exposure.

The standard tool for dealing with these complications is linear regression, and results are shown in Table 3. Here we consider monthly campaigns and hence there are 357 observations.

In regression (i) we regress cost per thousand on audience size and month (to correct for seasonality), and find the coefficient on audience size, 0.59, to be large and significant. Adding the demographic and cumulative exposure variables in regression (ii) brings this coefficient down to 0.25, but this is still economically as well as statistically significant: because audience size has a mean of 6.11 million and a standard deviation of 2.59 million and a typical cost per thousand is around $5 to $6, increasing audience size by one standard deviation increases cost per thousand by 10 to 15 percent. The demographic categories are fairly self-explanatory (urban represents counties belonging to the twenty-five largest metropolitan areas, and semiurban represents roughly all other counties that have population over 150,000); some of the demographic categories Nielsen reports, such as household size and presence of children, are left out because adding them changes little. The demographic variables are all in terms of percentage of the campaign's total audience belonging to that group; for example, a typical advertiser is willing to pay 16 cents more per thousand to reach an audience which is composed of 11 percent working women as opposed to 10 percent working women. Of the demographic categories, advertisers seem willing to pay extra for working women, middle-aged men, and households with incomes

TABLE 3

Regressions of Average Cost per Thousand on Average Audience Size, Demographic Characteristics, Four-Week Reach, and Social Good

Average Cost per Thousand (dollars) Regressed On:	(i)	(ii)	(iii)	(iv)
Social good			4.29***	1.17***
Average audience size (millions)	0.59***	0.25***		
Working women		0.16*		0.42***
Women 18–34		−0.06		−0.13*
Women 35–49		−0.03		−0.27*
Women ≥ 50		0.02		0.06
Men 18–34		0.13*		0.03
Men 35–49		0.29*		0.37**
Men ≥ 50		−0.08		−0.25***
Income > $60,000		0.40***		0.36***
East central		−0.08		−0.14
West central		0.12		0.04
South		−0.08		−0.13*
Pacific		0.06		0.19**
Urban		−0.05		−0.12*
Semiurban		0.08		0.09
Pay cable		−0.19**		−0.11
Basic cable		0.04		0.26***
Four-week reach		−0.0001		−0.0015
February	−0.98**	−0.72***	−1.49***	−0.73***
July	0.77*	0.88***	−0.45	0.30
Intercept	2.37***	0.22	5.89***	0.93
R^2	0.33	0.84	0.36	0.83

***Significant at $p = 0.001$; **significant at $p = 0.01$; *significant at $p = 0.05$.

greater than $60,000. The coefficient on four-week reach is small and not statistically significant.

Regressions (iii) and (iv) consider a dummy variable for social good (1 if social, 0 if not) instead of audience size. The results are that producers of social goods are willing to pay significantly more per thousand ($1.17, around 20 percent

more) after correcting for demographics; cumulative exposure is not important.

A third possible explanation is that people who rarely
watch television tend to watch the most popular shows. Because only popular shows manage to reach these people,
popular shows can command a higher price, and producers
of social brands might be willing to pay a premium to reach
them. However, this does not seem to be the case, as illustrated in Figure 10, which for each of the 357 monthly campaigns plots total cost versus four-week reach. It is true that
reaching remaining households is exponentially costly, but it
is also true that producers of social brands are consistently
willing to pay more, at all levels of cumulative exposure.

A fourth possible explanation is that advertisers of social
brands simply need to advertise more than advertisers of
nonsocial brands; because the total number of commercial
slots is limited, advertisers of social brands are forced to buy
the more expensive programs. Average cost per thousand

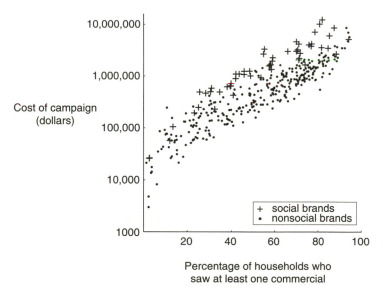

Figure 10. Total cost of campaign versus four-week reach.

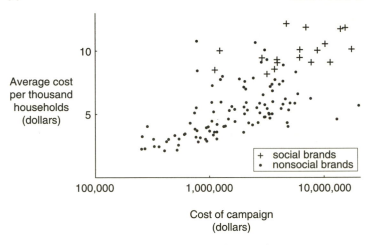

Figure 11. Cost per thousand versus total cost of campaign.

versus the total cost of the campaign over the year for each of the 119 brands is shown in Figure 11. This confirms the prediction (e.g., in Becker 1991, p. 1113) that social brands are in general more heavily advertised than nonsocial brands. But the graph shows that many nonsocial brands spend comparable amounts on advertising but still spend much less per household. In other words, social brands do not pay high cost per thousands simply because they advertise heavily.

There are several other plausible explanations. Popular shows might be more interesting and hence viewers might recall the commercials better (Webster and Lichty 1991). Advertising expensively on a popular show might indicate a higher-quality product (Nelson 1974, Kihlstrom and Riordan 1984, Milgrom and Roberts 1986). Because there are relatively few popular shows, networks might be in a better bargaining position when negotiating with advertisers over these shows and can thus charge higher prices. Popular shows might simply be more persuasive, better at changing preferences toward purchase (Dixit and Norman 1978). The audience size and demographics of popular shows might be more predictable, which would appeal to risk-averse advertisers (Fournier and Martin 1983). All of these explanations can explain why popular shows are more expensive per viewer but not why social goods tend to be advertised on expensive popular shows. In other words, there is no obvious reason why issues such as recall, quality, persuasion, and risk aversion apply more to social goods than to nonsocial ones.

The main problem with our analysis is that our sample of social goods is so limited, dominated by male-oriented products and beer in particular. As we have seen, we can correct for this to some extent, but there remains the possibility that instead of describing a social-good effect, we are simply describing a beer drinker effect. The only way to settle this convincingly is to look at data wherever available on other social goods, especially those with different demographic characteristics such as shoes, clothing, and soft drinks.

Another more conceptual problem is that it is difficult to distinguish whether a person buys a good because he expects that others will buy it or more simply because he knows that other people know about it. For example, Master Lock advertised on the Super Bowl for twenty consecutive years, spending most of its 1991 advertising budget for example on a single spot of a lock surviving a gunshot (Amos 1991). When buying a lock, I care not so much that others buy the same brand but rather that other people, including would-be thieves, think that the lock is tough. Instead of triggering coordination, publicity might simply be another aspect of the product (Becker and Murphy 1993; Keller 1993, p. 4).

Determining independently whether a good is social or not is also difficult. The general idea, however, of a distinction between public and nonpublic activities has been found to be empirically useful in studies by Anna Harvey (1999) and Juliet Schor (1998). Harvey finds that rates of partisan affiliation in the United States—measured by asking a person whether she considers herself to be a member of a political

party, or whether she cares which party wins, for example —
tend to be higher in states in which people can publicly register their party affiliation when they register to vote. This
suggests that partisanship is a coordination problem; if partisanship were mainly about, for example, individual loyalty,
then party registration laws should not make a difference.
Schor looks at women's cosmetics and finds that women are
more likely to buy expensive "status brands" of cosmetics
that are used in public, such as lipstick, and are less likely to
buy status brands of cosmetics which are used in private,
such as facial cleansers.

Our finding that popular shows are more expensive per
viewer is similar to results from data not across shows but
across localities. Fisher, McGowan, and Evans (1980) find
that local television station revenue increases not only in the
total number of households viewing but also in the square of
the total number of households viewing. Similarly, Ottina
(1995, p. 7) finds that the larger the local television market,
the more advertising revenue is generated per household.
Wirth and Bloch (1985, p. 136) find that the rates charged
by local stations for a spot on the program *MASH* increase
more than linearly in the number of viewing households.
Again, there are many possible explanations, including differences in audience demographics and stations' market
power across localities. Our data have fewer problems in
picking up a pure nonlinearity because they come from the
same nationwide viewing audience and advertising market
and include complete demographic and cumulative exposure
measures.

As mentioned before, several explanations are compatible
with the finding that popular shows are more expensive per
viewer. By showing also that advertisers of social goods buy
slots on more popular shows at a significant premium, we
are able to point to the specific explanation that more popular shows generate common knowledge and hence are better
at solving coordination problems. In any case, at least we
can say that our argument is empirically testable and not just
a logical nicety.

Strong Links and Weak Links

An important resource for a group's coordination is the pattern of social relationships among its members. In his discussion of "social capital," James Coleman (1988) cites as an example the "study circles" of South Korean student activists that form the basis for mobilizing demonstrations (for details, see Lee 2000). James Scott (1990, p. 151) notes that "the social coordination evident in traditional crowd action is achieved by the informal networks of community that join members of the subordinate group . . . through kinship, labor exchange, neighborhood, ritual practices, or daily occupational links." Roger Gould (1995, pp. 18–20) explicitly describes both rebellion as a coordination problem and common knowledge as forming through social relations: "Potential recruits to a social movement will only participate if they see themselves as part of a collectivity that is sufficiently large and solidary to assure some chance of success through mobilization. A significant source of the information they need to make this judgement is . . . social relations [that are] the mechanism for mutual recognition of shared interests (and of recognition of this recognition, and so on)."

However, a puzzle has come up in several contexts, having to do with the relative effectiveness of "strong" and "weak" links. The distinction between strong and weak links is an early insight of social network theory (Granovetter 1973). Roughly speaking, a strong link joins close friends and a weak link joins acquaintances. A general empirical finding (Rapoport and Horvath 1961) is that strong links tend to traverse a society "slowly": start with an arbitrary person, find two of her close friends, then find two close friends of each of these two people, and continue in this manner. As you iterate, the group increases slowly because often no one new is added: the close friends of my close friends tend to be my close friends also. If instead you successively add two acquaintances, the group grows quickly: the acquaintances of my acquaintances tend not to be my acquaintances. Weak links traverse a society "quickly": a demonstration suggests that any two people in the United States can be connected by as few as six weak links (Milgram 1992; see also Kochen 1989). Weak links tend to scatter widely, whereas strong links tend to be local, involuted. To connect a large society, then, weak links are more important than strong links; weak links are more important for spreading information (Granovetter 1995; see also Montgomery 1991). Examples of a strong-link network and a weak-link network, each with thirty people, are shown in Figure 12, where each person is represented by a point and the arrows indicate the direction of the flow of information.

In both networks, each person receives information from three friends, and hence both networks have the same "density," the same total number of links. In the strong-link network, a friend of a friend is likely to be a friend, whereas in the weak-link network, this is unlikely. Correspondingly, communication is slower in the strong-link network in that as you get information from friends, then friends of friends, then friends of friends of friends, and so on, even by the fourth iteration, you still only get information from about one-third of the people. In the weak-link network, by four interations you get information from almost everyone.

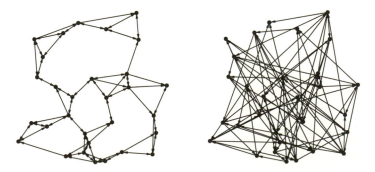

Figure 12. Strong links and weak links.

If coordinated action relies on communication, then because communication is faster in weak-link networks, it seems that weak-link networks should be better (see also Gould 1993, Macy 1991, and Marwell and Oliver 1993). The puzzle is that most evidence suggests that strong links are more important. Doug McAdam looks at data from volunteers in the 1964 Mississippi Freedom Summer and finds that the presence of a strong link to another potential participant correlates strongly and positively with participation, whereas the presence of a weak link has no correlation (McAdam 1986, McAdam and Paulsen 1993; see also Fernandez and McAdam 1988). In three classic "diffusion" studies, which look at individuals choosing whether to adopt a new technology, rates of adoption are actually negatively correlated with the presence of weak links (Valente 1995, p. 51).

One way to deal with the puzzle is simply to say that strong links do not operate through communication but through a completely different mechanism, such as social influence: "although weak links may be more effective as diffusion channels, strong ties embody greater potential for influencing behavior" (McAdam 1986, p. 80). This claim is, of course, reasonable, and social relations are undoubtedly conduits for several different things, including information, influence, and feelings. However, our argument, which emphasizes the importance of common knowledge, shows that strong links can be better even in terms of communication alone. In other words, strong links can be demonstrably better without resorting to mechanisms other than communication (for more details, see Chwe 1999b, 2000).

To see this, take a simple example. Say we have four people, and say that each person has a "threshold" of three; that is, each person is willing to participate in the group action as long as three people in total do so. Consider two networks, the "square" and "kite," as shown in Figure 13, where all links are symmetric (communication flows in both directions). Say that before deciding to participate, each person

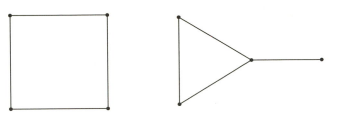

Figure 13. Square and kite.

communicates her willingness to participate, her threshold, with her neighbors. In the square, each person knows that there are three people with thresholds of three: himself and his two neighbors. That is, each person knows that there is enough collective sentiment to make group action possible. But say I'm considering whether to participate. What do I know about, say, my right-hand neighbor? I know that he has a threshold of three. I am his neighbor, and hence I know that he knows I have a threshold of three. But I do not know anything about his other neighbor "across" from me, who might not want to participate at all, in which case my neighbor to the right will surely not participate. Hence I cannot count on my right-hand neighbor to participate. Hence I do not participate. So even though it is a fact that there is enough sentiment to make group action possible, and everyone knows it, no one participates. Coordination fails because no one knows that anyone else knows: the fact is not common knowledge.

In the kite, each individual in the "triangle" knows similarly that his two neighbors have thresholds of three. But here, each individual knows that his two neighbors know the thresholds of each other. Among the three people in the triangle, the fact that there are three people with thresholds of three is not only known by each person; each person knows that each other person knows this fact. Thus the three members of the "triangle" participate, and coordination is successful (at least partially — the fourth person, not in the "triangle," does not partcipate).

So, in this example, the kite is better than the square. This difference cannot be accounted for by summary characteristics such as the total number of links (four in both cases), or even by finer measures such as the number of neighbors each person has (in the kite, two of the participants have only two neighbors, as in the square). The difference between the square and kite is truly a difference in the kind of structure. In the kite, each member of the triangle participates because she knows that her friends know each other.

But this is exactly the advantage of strong links in general. If you and I are potential participants connected by a strong link, your friends are likely to be my friends, and the eagerness to participate among our group of friends would be common knowledge among us. If you and I are connected by a weak link, I don't know your friends and you don't know mine. In other words, the idea that weak links are always better for communication relies on the assumption that communication is about "first order" knowledge only and not about knowledge of what others know. Weak links might be better for communicating widely, but strong links are better at forming common knowledge locally. When there is no issue of coordinated action and hence common knowledge, weak links are better: for example, weak links are better for finding out about job opportunities (Granovetter 1995). For social coordination, however, strong links have an advantage.

In an expanded analysis, McAdam and Ronnelle Paulsen (1993, p. 658) find that organizations such as religious groups and civil rights groups give individuals "a highly salient identity and strong social support for activism based on that identity." Interestingly, when organizational affiliation and the presence of a strong tie are both included in the analysis, the strong positive effect of strong ties disappears. But organizational affiliation and strong ties may simply be indicators of the same underlying "variable": belonging to a group among which wanting to participate is common knowledge. Empirical studies of collective action are often based on surveys: for example, when Karl-Dieter Opp and

Christiane Gern (1993) surveyed participants in the demonstrations that led to the collapse of East Germany, they simply asked each person whether he had friends who participated and found that this was a significant variable in predicting his participation. One way to verify the importance of strong links, and common knowledge, would be to also ask each person if his friends who participated knew each other.

We often think of coordinated action arising out of communities or "subcultures." But what makes a community? If we apply the logic of common knowledge, then a community is not like a city center, in which each person has many scattered relationships, but more like a neighborhood, in which each person might have fewer friends but in which one's friends tend to know each other.

The Chapel in the Panopticon

Jeremy Bentham, often considered one of the founders of rational choice theory, also came up with the "panopticon" prison design, describing it in meticulous detail and lobbying for it ceaselessly for more than twenty years (Semple 1993). The design, which arranges prison cells in a circle around a central guard tower, was not implemented in Bentham's lifetime and has had limited influence on actual prison construction. Recently it has had greater success as an analogy: "the diagram of a mechanism of power reduced to its ideal form," according to Michel Foucault (1979, p. 205). The panopticon structures visibility in three ways: a guard can see all prisoners from a single vantage point, guards can see prisoners without being seen, and prisoners cannot see each other. Hence the panopticon places prisoners' cells in a circle around the central "inspector's lodge," the inspector's lodge has window blinds and smoked glass preventing anyone from seeing inside, and "protracted partitions" separating the prisoners' cells are extended inward to block prisoners' sight lines. Here I refer to these features as centrality, asymmetry, and separation. The panopticon's operating logic is usually considered brutally obvious. But it is not clear which of the three features are most important or even necessary, and how exactly they operate. What makes a panopticon a panopticon?

Bentham himself in his original letters downplays separation: "The essence of it consists, then, in the *centrality* of the inspector's situation, combined with the well-known and most effectual contrivances for *seeing without being seen*"; later in his postscripts, Bentham states explicitly that the protracted partitions are not necessary (Bentham [1791] 1843, p. 44). Bentham aggresively promoted the panopticon as applying not only to prisons but also to social institutions at large, including hospitals, schools, and factories; in some of these cases, Bentham ([1791] 1843, p. 60) makes clear that both asymmetry and separation are optional. In Unit F at Stateville Correctional Center in Joliet, Illinois, one of the few panopticon prison houses in use in the United States, there is only centrality: prisoners can move about and talk, and even when confined to their cells can see each other; the central guard tower is open and the guards inside are clearly visible, as shown in Figure 14 (see also Foucault 1979, plate 6).

The purpose of separation is straightforward: to prevent prisoners from communicating and thereby prevent coordinated action. According to Bentham ([1791] 1843, p. 46), "overpowering the guards requries a union of hands, and a concert among minds. But what union, or what concert, can there be among persons, none of whom will have set eyes on any other from the first moment of his entrance?" According to Foucault (1979, p. 200), "this invisibility is a guarantee of order. If the inmates are convicts, there is no danger of a plot, an attempt at collective escape."

The purpose of centrality seems mainly to be efficiency: fewer guards are necessary, and labor costs are lower (see Rendon 1998 on Los Angeles County's recent Twin Towers maximum-security prison). Asymmetry also helps in cutting

Figure 14. Unit F, Stateville Correctional Center, Stateville, Illinois.

costs; because a prisoner can never tell if he is being watched, he has to act as if he is being watched constantly. The panopticon, however, is not meant to be just an exercise in cost cutting, but the archetype of an entirely different kind of power. Here asymmetry seems to be the crucial issue: as explained by Nancy Fraser (1989, p. 23), the panopticon was the prototype of "micropractices linking new processes of production of new knowledges to new kinds of power. . . . This link depended upon the asymmetrical character of the gaze: it was unidirectional — the scientist or warden could see the inmate but not vice versa. . . . Because the unidirectionality of visibility denied the inmates knowledge of when and whether they were actually being watched, it made them internalize the gaze and in effect surveil themselves."

According to Foucault (1979, p. 202), asymmetry "dissociat[es] the see/being seen dyad" of guard and prisoner. But this dyadic analysis is incomplete in that it does not consider how prisoners know about, and might communicate with, each other. It turns out that asymmetry has another important function (which it shares with separation): preventing the formation of common knowledge and hence coordinated action among prisoners.

The evidence for this claim is a design feature that Foucault, and most other observers since, largely ignore: Bentham ([1791] 1843, p. 47) devotes an entire section in his postscripts on how one of the advantages of centrality is that it allows a chapel to be placed above the inspector's lodge. This allows prisoners to "receive the benefits of divine service . . . without stirring from their cells. No thronging or jostling in the way between the scene of work and the scene destined to devotion; no quarrellings, or confederatings, nor plottings to escape; nor yet any whips and fetters to prevent it." In Bentham's diagram, shown in Figure 15, the chapel

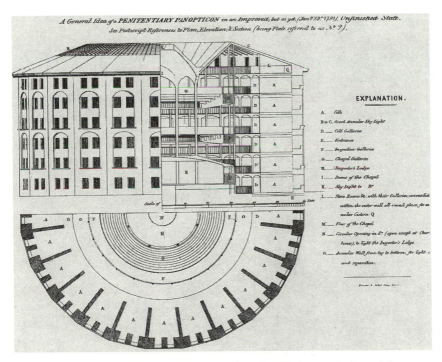

Figure 15. Bentham's panopticon: chapel galleries are indicated by G and the chapel floor is indicated by M.

galleries (where Bentham planned for respectable visitors to sit and join the convicts in devotion) and the chapel floor are clearly shown.

So the panopticon as envisioned by Bentham was not completely an instrument of surveillance but also a ritual structure. Prisoners were not only the objects of surveillance but also an audience, in at least a limited sense. It just so happens (and, for Bentham, this is one of the panopticon's advantages) that centrality, which makes surveillance easy, also makes ritual easy. If separation were dropped, as Bentham does in his postscript, the only thing differentiating the chapel and the inspector's lodge, the only thing keeping the panopticon from becoming a theater in the round, is asymmetry.

So asymmetry not only affects the dyadic relationship between observer and observed; it is also essential for keeping the observed from implicitly comunicating, from forming common knowledge. Say, for example, that the central guard tower was open and visible to all prisoners. Then, if a central guard were visibly sleeping or somehow disabled or killed, or if the central tower were visibly overtaken by prisoners, there would be an electric common knowledge and hence riotous effect; each prisoner would know that other prisoners could see the same thing. In a prison without centrality, say with dispersed guard towers and cells, there would be much less danger of an incident at a single location becoming a public signal. This is not just a theoretical concern: Joseph Ragen, the warden at Stateville from 1936 to 1961, "points out to visitors that while it is true that the guard in the tower can see every prisoner, it is also true that every prisoner can see the guard—and can see when his back is turned. So, while he uses the towers, he also places guards at other strategic points in these cell houses" (Erickson 1957, p. 22; see also Webster and Phalen 1997, p. 119, on the mass audience as "reversed" panopticon). In this way the panopticon is unstable: the price of surveillance efficiency is a structure that is easily "invertible."

Why is the chapel, obvious in Bentham's design, absent from Foucault's interpretation? Is there anything at stake in this omission? Foucault writes that for a single observer in the central tower, the prison cells are "like so many cages, so many small theatres, in which each actor is alone, perfectly individualized and constantly visible" (Foucault 1979, p. 200). This is misleading, if theater is considered a collective experience in which many people all watch, and have common knowledge of, the same thing. In contrast, Bentham ([1791] 1843, p. 45) says that the prisoners provide to the principal inspector, and his children living inside the central lodge, "that great and constant fund of entertainment to the sedentary and vacant in towns — the looking out of the window." For a few people looking out at a great variety of scenes and objects, Bentham's analogy is more appropriate. One might say that by using the idea of theater to describe the guard's surveillance, Foucault draws attention away from the possibility that the panopticon might in fact be a theater for the prisoners. Similarly, Foucault (1979, p. 203) speculates that Bentham may have been inspired by Le Vaux's menagerie at Versailles, in which a single room looked out into seven cages, each with different animal species. But the only similarity between this menagerie and the panopticon is centrality (presumably there was no need to prevent animals from seeing each other or looking back at visitors). This analogy avoids the issue of common knowledge formation among the observed and hence the panopticon's instability, because presumably animals are not capable of coordinating a joint escape attempt.

Foucault's overall aim is to establish a historical shift from an older kind of power based on ritual and ceremony to a modern kind of power exemplified by the panopticon; through the panoptic principle, "a whole type of society emerges. Antiquity had been a civilization of spectacle. 'To render accessible to a multiple of men the inspection of a small number of objects': this was the problem to which the architecture of temples, theatres and circuses responded. . . . The modern age poses the opposite problem: 'To procure for a small number, or even for a single individual, the instantaneous view of a great multitude.' . . . Our society is not one of spectacle, but of surveillance. . . . We are neither in the amphitheatre or the stage, but in the panoptic machine" (Foucault 1979, pp. 216–17; quotations from Julius 1831). Regardless of whether one accepts Foucault's broad argument, if the panopticon were acknowledged to have a ritual structure built into its very center, then it would not be as singular an example. One of Foucault's historical reasons for why mechanisms of power abandoned spectacle in favor of surveillance is the instability of spectacle: public executions, for example, could switch suddenly from rituals of state order to riots against it. But the panopticon has a similar instability, immediately turning into a stadium were it not for smoked glass and window blinds.

Even without a chapel, the panopticon still has a ritual aspect; the chapel just makes it more obvious. Bentham ([1791] 1843, p. 45) states that its "fundamental advantages . . . [are] the *apparent omnipresence* of the inspector (if devines will allow me the expression,) combined with the extreme facility of his *real presence*." It is not just that each prisoner is under surveillance; each prisoner knows, it is "apparent," that the surveillance is omnipresent, that everyone else is under similar surveillance. According to Foucault (1979, p. 201), "the inmate will have constantly before his eyes the tall outline of the central tower from which he is spied upon." In other words, Nancy Fraser's (1989, p. 23) idea that "panoptical surveillance . . . keeps a low profile [with] no need of the spectacular displays characteristic of the exercise of power in the *ancient régime*" is not quite correct; the central tower is not invisible but continuously present, even iconic. The "high tower, powerful and knowing" sounds a lot like "the body of the king, with its strange material and physical presence" (Foucault 1979, p. 208), which is supposed to be the panopticon's exact opposite. Foucault (1979, pl. 4) even includes a picture of (as described by the caption) "a prisoner, in his cell, kneeling at prayer before the central inspection tower."

If communication is thought of in terms of directional flows, then a royal festival (a multitude seeing a single person) does seem the direct opposite of the panopticon (a single person seeing a multitude). If, however, we think in terms of common knowledge formation among the multitude, which I argue is the crucial issue in a festival anyhow, then the festival and panopticon are more similar than different. The festival achieves common knowledge through intensity of image, feeling, and interaction, whereas the panopticon achieves it through sensory deprivation: each person cannot see anything except the looming omnipresent inspection tower, and it is immediately evident to each prisoner from the panopticon's architecture that all prisoners see it alone and nothing else. In a panopticon, prisoners are separated but not atomized in the sense of being scattered, each with his own private experience; the mode of surveillance itself is common knowledge. To achieve the kind of surveillance that Fraser describes, each person would have to feel a lonely paranoia, that his surveillance is his alone, unsure if anyone else is being treated similarly. Bentham's panopticon, and Foucault's, do not do this.

3

Elaborations

Competing Explanations

Here I briefly discuss two competing kinds of explanations in contrast to ours. One way by which rituals are thought to influence behavior is through direct psychological stimulation. For example, "rhythmic or repetitive behavior coordinates the limbic discharges (that is, affective states) of a group of conspecifics. It can generate a level of arousal that is both pleasurable and reasonably uniform among the individuals so that necessary group action is facilitated" (d'Aquili and Laughlin 1979, p. 158). This can very well be the case but, as remarked earlier, cannot be the whole story because, if it were, a ritual would not have to be a collective event; each person could simply be aroused individually and separately. Our argument relies on each person not just being in a similar emotional or mental state, but each person being aware of others and aware of others' awareness, which is not captured if one thinks only in terms of how a single organism responds to stimuli. Putting this another way, according to Eugene d'Aquili and Charles Laughlin (1979, p. 158), "the simplest paradigm to explain the situation in man [during ritual] is the feeling of union that occurs during orgasm . . . [in which] there is intense simultaneous discharge from both of the autonomic subsystems. We are postulating that the various ecstasy states that can be produced in man after exposure to rhythmic auditory, visual, or tactile stimuli produce a feeling of union with other members participating in that ritual." The physiological effects of orgasm undeniably can help in establishing a close and intimate connection with another person, but orgasms often occur with little or no emotional connection or even alone.

Another kind of explanation is based on how being physically together in a group of people affects individual emotions. In extreme form, this is the idea behind "mob psychology" or "crowd psychology," which persists in the popular imagination despite being rejected by empirical observation: for example, even in situations like the "Who concert stampede" in Cincinnati, Ohio, in which eleven people were killed, crushed by a crowd trying to enter Riverfront Coliseum, there was very little evidence of "ruthless competition" and mass panic, and lots of evidence of cooperative, helping behavior (Johnson 1987; see also Turner and Killian 1987 and Curtis and Aguirre 1993). Being in a large group of people does, of course, affect one's feelings and thus actions, depending on the situation. Richard A. Berk (1974, p. 361) follows a spontaneous, unplanned demonstration against the Vietnam War in extremely fine detail, noting that after three students started to build a barricade blocking a major thoroughfare, "students at the barricade responded by beginning many simultaneous 'negotiations.' Various proposals were made and debated: 'This barricade stuff is stupid and risky because it is destruction of property. Why don't we just stage a sit-down here in the street instead?' 'What you guys are doing is too risky. You'll be arrested or suspended. I know it's just not worth that much to me.'" After the barricade was built, "250 students were milling around, many still arguing. An active minority strongly endorsed the barricade. A smaller though equally active minority opposed it. Most students seemed undecided but eventually chose temporarily to support the barricade, or at least to let it stand." In this case at least, the fact of being together in a crowd did not at all seem to unite the demonstrators in a common euphoria or emotion; if anything, what the physical closeness of the crowd made possible were discussions over tactics, costs, and benefits.

The feelings that come from being together are important in rituals and other group events; one disadvantage, however, of considering them as a principal or defining aspect is that certain practices that are fairly evidently rituals do not involve physical togetherness. Daniel Dayan and Elihu Katz (1992, p. 145) find televised media events to be similar to the Passover seder, which "has served through the ages as a powerful means of unification, offering a ceremonial structure that takes account of geographic dispersion by translating a monumental occasion into a multiplicity of simultaneous, similarly programmed, home-bound microevents while focused, however, on a symbolic center." Benedict Anderson (1991, p. 145) asks us to consider "national anthems, for example, sung on national holidays. . . . Singing the Marseillaise, Waltzing Matilda, and Indonesia Raya provide occasions for unisonality, for the echoed physical realization of the imagined community. . . . How selfless this unisonance feels! If we are aware that others are singing these songs precisely when and as we are, we have no idea who they may be, or even where, out of earshot, they are singing. Nothing connects us at all but imagined sound." Even if I sing the national anthem alone in my room, I can still have strong feelings of unity based on nothing more than my knowing that other people are also doing it. This alone can create what Anderson calls the "imagined community"; singing together in the same room is just its "physical realization." Singing separately still qualifies as a ceremony even without any of Durkheim's (1912 [1995], p. 220) "collective effervescence," simply because each person knows that others are joining in.

Is Common Knowledge an Impossible Ideal?

The most obvious problem with the concept of common knowledge is that it seems to require great cognitive abilities: can anyone think through, say, more than two or three layers of "I know that she knows that he knows . . ."? Common knowledge thus seems to be an ideal, impractical concept. For example, Ariel Rubinstein (1989) gives an example in which two people have ninety-nine levels of metaknowledge but cannot coordinate because they do not have the hundredth. There are various ways of making the concept of common knowledge less strict and more plausible. Instead of requiring that I know that you know, one can require that I believe with 90 percent probability that you believe with 90 percent probability and so on (Monderer and Samet 1989; Morris, Rob, and Shin 1995; Morris 1999). One can also define common knowledge not as a condition on arbitrarily many levels, but on a recursive step, which is more plausible as an actual thought process (see Lewis 1969, p. 52; also, e.g., Milgrom 1981): assume that when we make eye contact, we both know that we are making eye contact. When we make eye contact, I know that we are making eye contact, and hence I know that you know that we are making eye contact, and so forth.

Perhaps the most plausible way of dealing with this issue, as pointed out by Herbert Clark and Catherine Marshall (1992, p. 33), is to say that people recognize common knowledge and deviations from it heuristically: "if A and B make certain assumptions about each other's rationality, they can use certain states of affairs as a basis for *inferring* the infinity of conditions all at once." When we make eye contact, I don't have to think through anything; I can simply infer from past experience that usually when we make eye contact, common knowledge is formed.

To take a specific example, the video conferencing system at Rank Xerox's EuroParc research lab was originally designed so that each person had a video camera and monitor. But a female EuroParc psychologist noticed the following problem when linked to a male colleague: "We were both changing for jujitsu and he covered his lens with his jacket so it blanked out my view of his office. I wasn't thinking and assumed that because I couldn't see him, he couldn't see me. I forgot my camera was still on" (McCrone 1994). The psychologist's error was in misjudging the situation, confusing the video conferencing situation with the everyday face-to-face meeting situation, not in incorrectly parsing the layers of "I know that he knows that. . . ." The video conferencing system's designer's error was in assuming that communication is only about transferring messages from one person to another, first-order knowledge. After this episode, the system was redesigned to include a "confidence" monitor, which displays to each person their own outgoing signal, but this is not an unambiguous improvement toward approximating face-to-face communication, in which you can see the other person's eyes and thus see if he is seeing you. The confidence monitor can help you avoid embarrassing moments, but it still doesn't help you know when the other person is looking at you.

Thus even people who design and test new communication systems do not as a matter of course think through layers of metaknowledge when placed in unaccustomed situations. We know that common knowledge is formed by meeting face-to-face, and other similar situations, out of experience. I stop at a red traffic light out of habit, but a fully specified argument for doing so would involve an infinite regress: I stop because I think that other people are going, and I think that other people are going because I think that they think that I am stopping, and so on.

Another way to see how common knowledge is part of the "real world" is from the perspective of cognition. For example, experimental psychologists ask children questions like "Does John know that Mary knows where the ice-cream van is?" and find that children roughly of a certain age (around seven years old) reliably answer but younger children do not (Perner and Wimmer 1985). Chimpanzees can follow the gaze of other chimpanzees and humans but, when begging for food, do not seem to distinguish between a person with a blindfold over her eyes (who obviously cannot see the begging gesture) and a person with a blindfold over her mouth (Povinelli and O'Neill 2000). William S. Horton and Boaz Keysar (1996, p. 94) conduct an experiment that suggests that when a person initially plans an utterance, he does not take into account the listener's knowledge; common knowledge comes in later as "part of a correction mechanism that is part of the monitoring function," which might lead to the utterance's revision. Recent work in neuroscience suggests the existence of a "theory of mind module," possibly located in the orbitofrontal cortex of the brain, which enables people to understand the mental states of others; evidence suggests that autism involves an impairment of this module (Baron-Cohen 1995; see Brothers 1997 on the "social brain"). Thus common knowledge is not just an ideal but a concept that is subject to emprical investigation, not only at the level of social practices but also at the levels of psychology, evolutionary biology, and neuroscience.

Meaning and Common Knowledge

A central message of this book is that publicity — more precisely, common knowledge generation — as well as content must be considered in understanding cultural practices such as rituals. But although this distinction is useful analytically, content and publicity are never completely separable, and interestingly interact.

By separating content and publicity, we do gain a sometimes necessary flexibility. Daniel Boorstin (1961, pp. 5, 57–59) complains that *"the celebrity is a person who is known for his well-knownness.* . . . [T]he phrase 'By Appointment to His Majesty' was of course, a kind of use of the testimonial endorsement. But the King was in fact a great person, one of illustrious lineage and with impressive actual and symbolic powers. . . . He was not a mere celebrity." But as we have seen, a king's "actual" power is at least partly constituted by "pseudo-events" such as royal progresses: indeed, a pseudo-event is usually "intended to be a self-fulfilling prophecy" (Boorstin 1961, p. 12; see also Cowen 2000 on fame). Earlier "power draped itself in the outward garb of a mythical order"; today Guy Debord's ([1967] 1995, p. 20) "society of the spectacle" is "self-generated, and makes up its own rules: it is a specious form of the sacred." The point here is that sometimes it does not matter whether the content of a message is "true": Lewis (1969, p. 39) notes that "if yesterday I told you a story about people who got separated in the subway and happened to meet again at Charles Street, and today we get separated in the same way, we might independently decide to go and wait at Charles Street. It makes no difference whether the story I told you was true, or whether you thought it was, or whether I thought it was, or even whether I claimed it was. A fictive precedent would be as effective as an actual one."

But one reason that content and publicity cannot really be separated is simply that all communications have an assumed or implied audience. In John Austin's (1975) terminology, a speech act has not just a "locutionary" literal meaning, but also an "illocutionary" meaning having to do with the speaker's intentions in a given situation: for example, "Yes, I will marry you" has a different meaning when spoken in private than when spoken publicly in front of friends. Perhaps instead of saying that this book is about publicity as distinct from content, one might say that it is about one aspect of illocutionary meaning.

Content and publicity can interact in interesting ways. Sometimes content indicates the social situation, which includes considerations of publicity, in which it is to be understood: when a paperback best seller has "Over 5 million copies sold" on its cover, this sentence is part of the "text" of the book. The language in which a book is written indicates a presumed audience. Medieval Russian manuals for icon painters instructed that "the righthand part of the painting was thought of as the 'left', and conversely the left part of the painting as the 'right.' In other words the reckoning was not from our point of view (as spectators of the picture) but from the point of view of someone facing us, an internal observer imagined to be within the depicted world" (Uspensky 1975, p. 34). Here the content of the icon indicates the painter's understanding of the viewer's relationship to it.

Michael Fried characterizes some modern sculpture as "public" or "theatrical" on various grounds, including "objecthood." Theatrical sculpture emphasizes "wholeness, singleness and indivisibility . . . a work's being, as nearly as possible, 'one thing,' a single 'Specific Object'" (Fried 1967, pp. 12, 20). A good example is Tony Smith's *Die,* a six-foot cube. The meaning of an Anthony Caro sculpture, on the other hand, is in the "mutual and naked *juxtaposition* of the I-beams, girders, cylinders, lengths of piping, sheet metal and grill which it comprises rather than in the compound *object* which they compose." If "public" and "theatrical" are understood in terms of common knowledge, perhaps unitary objects are theatrical because each observer knows that others see it in a similar way; an observer looking at a sculpture with many interacting elements expects that others more likely see and understand it differently.

That single unitary images are better at generating common knowledge is also illustrated by the marketing of high-concept films. Justin Wyatt (1994, p. 112) compares print advertising for Steven Spielberg's *Jaws* and Robert Altman's *Nashville,* both from 1975: ads for *Jaws* featured a huge shark on the verge of eating a naked woman, while ads for *Nashville* showed each of the "cast of 24 characters emblazoned—patchwork style—on the back of a denim jacket." Wyatt notes that a "clean, bold image" is important because print ads mainly appear in newspapers, which have relatively poor print quality. But strong singular images also better create the necessary common knowledge. Wyatt sees the marketing strategy for *Jaws,* based on a single, striking image, as setting the pattern for all high-concept films to follow, while *Nashville,* according to its advertising copy "a story of lovers and laughers and losers and winners," was a relative box office failure, despite excellent reviews. Since then, the trend toward unitary marketing images has continued: even titles such as *Terminator 2* and *Independence Day* are abbreviated to *T2* and *ID4* (see also Cowen 2000, p. 17, and Wyatt 1994, p. 25).

Of course, the meaning of any single communication can only be fully understood in the context of a society's existing understandings. In 1964 Tony Schwartz created the "Daisy" spot, one of the most effective political television commercials of all time. The commercial starts with a girl's counting of daisy petals, which segues into a nuclear countdown and explosion, and ends with white lettering on a black background stating "Vote for President Johnson on November 3." According to Schwartz (1973, p. 93), the commercial "created a huge controversy. Many people, especially the Republicans, shouted that the spot accused Senator Goldwater [Johnson's Republican opponent] of being trigger-happy. But *nowhere in the spot is Goldwater mentioned*. There is not even an indirect reference to Goldwater. . . . Senator Goldwater had stated previously that he supported the use of tactical atomic weapons. The commercial *evoked* a deep feeling in many people that Goldwater might actually use nuclear weapons. This mistrust was not in the *Daisy* spot. It was in the people who viewed the commercial. The stimuli of the film and sound evoked these feelings and allowed people to express what they inherently believed." A viewer, realizing that her own fears about Goldwater were brought out by the ad, would also realize that other people must be reacting similarly; the ad thus brought this shared concern into the open, making it common knowledge. This was not solely because of the viewership of the commercial (it appeared on "Monday Night at the Movies"), or because of the "content" of the commercial itself, but, as Schwartz designed it, because of the way it interacted with people's existing understandings.

These considerations only scratch the surface. My understanding of how you understand a given communication depends on our shared symbol system and world view: Elizabeth Tudor's royal progress would not be understood as such by Hayam Wuruk's audience, and vice versa. David Laitin (1986) explains how in Nigeria in 1976, the issue of establishing a Federal Sharia Court of Appeal based on Islamic law threatened all-out religious conflict, even war. The Yoruba states in the western region of Nigeria, with population evenly divided between Christian and Muslim, were swing regions in this debate; however, Yoruba delegates took moderate positions and laid the grounds for national compromise. Laitin explains this in terms of hegemony: for

Yorubas, it is common sense that ancestral city, not religion, is the basis for political mobilization and conflict. A Yoruba Christian did not feel threatened by the Sharia issue because she knew that Yoruba Muslims would not understand it as a religious call to arms, and vice versa. The point here is that common knowledge depends crucially on how each person understands or interprets how other people understand or interpret a communication.

Contesting Common Knowledge

So far we have mainly discussed coordination as uncontested. But of course people disagree about how to coordinate. Russell Hardin (1995, p. 30) observes that state authority "depends on coordination at the level of government and on lack of coordination at the level of any potential popular opposition. The state need not compel everyone at gunpoint, it need merely make it in virtually everyone's clear interest *individually* to comply with the law even though collectively it might be their interest to oppose the law." Because people fight over coordinations, and common knowledge is helpful for coordination, people fight over mechanisms for generating common knowledge. To create Solidarity in Poland, "the organizing conversations at Cegielski [Railway Works] were conducted in places beyond the gaze of foremen — in trains and buses to and from work, in remote sections of the plant, at lunch breaks. . . . This space was not a gift; it had to be created by people who fought to create it" (Lawrence Goodwin, quoted in Scott 1990, p. 123). Or as microbroadcaster Napoleon Williams of Decatur, Illinois, notes, "You can buy a Uzi fully assembled, but it's illegal to buy [an FM transmitter] fully assembled in this country" (Burke 1997). Schelling ([1960] 1980, p. 144) writes that "the participants of a square dance may all be thoroughly dissatisfied with the particular dances being called, but as long as the caller has the microphone, nobody can dance anything else." The idea that fair and equal communicative capability is necessary for fair outcomes is basic enough to build a social theory on (Habermas 1989).

That people fight over common knowledge generation is an obvious point, but it helps in understanding the importance of cultural struggles. Sometimes cultural practices are seen as mostly superstructural: "In the case of American slavery, for instance, it is revealing to talk about the 'trappings' of master-class authority and about symbolic exchanges between blacks and whites. But there comes a point at which that translates a harsh condition into form and theater" (Walters 1980, p. 554). But "theater," understood more broadly as common knowledge generation, has real power. In the case of American slavery, the prohibition on teaching slaves how to read and write was not just one of the "trappings" of white rule but an attempt to suppress communication and hence rebellion; interestingly, the real power of the written word is in communicating publicly (putting up a sign) and over long distances (notes to slaves on other plantations); in face-to-face interactions, talking is easier. Even at the face-to-face level, "gatherings of five or more slaves without the presence of a white observer were universally forbidden" (Raboteau 1978, p. 53, quoted in Scott 1990). In turn slaves fought back, for example, by talking secretly in "hush arbors" and placing hidden meanings in publicly sung spirituals ("Canaan" meant the North and freedom [Scott 1990, p. 116]); this fight was not merely "symbolic" but was a struggle for the communications infrastructure that would help in real coordinated actions, such as escape attempts.

In his autobiographical novel *Black Boy,* Richard Wright (1945 [1993], pp. 235–37) tells how he and another employee, Harrison, were manipulated by Mr. Olin, a white foreman. "Harrison and I knew each other casually, but there had never been the slightest trouble between us. . . . 'Do you know Harrison?'. . . . Mr. Olin said in a low, confidential tone. 'A little while ago I went down to get a Coca-Cola and Harrison was waiting for you at the door of the building with a knife. . . . Said he was going to get you. Said you called him a dirty name. Now, we don't want any fight-ing or bloodshed on the job.' . . . 'I've got to see that boy and talk to him,' I said, thinking out loud. 'No, you'd better not,' Mr. Olin said. 'You'd better let some of us white boys talk to him.'" Later Wright found Harrison alone in the basement. "'Say, Harrison, what's this all about?' I asked, standing cautiously four feet from him. . . . 'I'm not angry with you.' 'Shucks, I thought *you* was looking for me to cut me,' Harrison explained. 'Mr. Olin, he came over here this morning and said you was going to kill me with a knife the moment you saw me. He said you was mad at me because I had insulted you. But I ain't said nothing about you.' . . . [H]e stammered and pulled from his pocket a long, gleaming knife; it was already open. . . . 'You were going to cut me?' I asked. 'If you had cut me, I was gonna cut you first,' he said." Here Wright and Harrison face a coordination prob-lem: each person wants to be peaceful only if the other is also peaceful. Neither person is angry, but Harrison carries a knife because he does not know whether Wright is angry. In fact, even if he knew that Wright is not angry, Harrison might carry a knife if he were unsure about whether Wright knows that he is not angry. To solve this coordination prob-lem, common knowledge is necessary, and this is what is pre-vented by Mr. Olin's restricting communication, so that only white boys talk. Wright's parable is not only about the deceit of whites but of the fundamental need for blacks to have an undistorted "public sphere."

It is often remarked that people such as Gandhi and Mar-tin Luther King Jr. when coordinating public demonstrations had an expert sense of theater. In the United States in the 1990s, the organization ACT UP (Aids Coalition to Unleash Power) followed in this tradition, transforming the rituals of weddings and funerals into political statements (e.g., by scat-tering the ashes of loved ones who died from AIDS on the White House lawn) and by disrupting almost any public space imaginable, including (in New York City alone) Grand Central Station, the New York Stock Exchange, St. Patrick's Cathedral, Shea Stadium, and any number of press confer-

ences and political fund raisers. One notable thing about
ACT UP was that its volunteer media committee was staffed
by television producers, journalists, public relations experts,
and advertising agency art directors (Signorile 1993); if Gandhi could rely on a sense of theater, ACT UP could rely on
the techniques of professional advertising.

In 1984, introducing its new Macintosh computer in the
face of complete market dominance by the IBM personal
computer, Apple Computer's television commercial naturally
played off George Orwell's *Nineteen Eighty-Four, A Novel.*
A female hammer thrower wearing the colorful Macintosh
logo enters an auditorium in which rows of grey zombies
stare at Big Brother on a massive television screen; as Big
Brother exclaims "We shall prevail," the hammer flies and
shatters the screen; the open-mouthed audience gapes into
the explosive wind. The text and voice-over then explain
that "On January 24th, Apple Computer will introduce
Macintosh. And you'll see why 1984 won't be like '1984'"
(Rutherford 1994, pp. 140–41). Here the Macintosh hammer destroys the mechanism of publicity. In other words, Big
Brother is not vanquished and replaced on the telescreen by
a Macintosh; rather, the Macintosh destroys the communications technology that makes Big Brother possible. However,
the destruction is itself a public event (we are shown explicitly the zombies' reaction to it); it's an explosion, not a
power outage (in which you don't know at first whether
your neighbors are also affected). This ambiguity is also evident in Apple's appealing to nonconformists but, at the same
time, airing the commercial on the Super Bowl, an irony ap-
preciated by the trade magazine *Advertising Age:* "Apple
gave birth to Macintosh with the sort of smoke and mirrors
that would make Big Brother proud" (Johnson 1994).

Thus it may be more effective to harness rather than at-
tack the Super Bowl's publicity. Three days before the 1993
Super Bowl, domestic violence activists held a press conference presenting anecdotal evidence that more husbands beat
their wives after the Super Bowl than on an average day; the
group called not for a boycott but for NBC to donate Super

Bowl air time to discuss domestic violence. NBC supplied thirty seconds in the pregame show; the public service announcement, which showed a man in a jail cell, made no reference to football (Gorov 1993, Lipsyte 1993). Still, the impact of this announcement was best evidenced by the flurry of newspaper articles attacking it (notably Ringle 1993; see also Cohen and Solomon 1993).

The point here is that simply by airing it on the Super Bowl, activists put domestic violence on the national agenda more publicly than ever before. They gave the issue an enduring "hook," republicized or at least recalled every year (e.g., Isaacson 1996). Their strategy echoed the August 1968 protest of the Miss America Pageant, in which a "Women's Liberation" banner disrupted the live television broadcast and the throwing of bras, false eyelashes, and *Cosmopolitan* into a Freedom Trash Can was improperly immortalized in the media-invented phrase of "bra-burning" (Morgan 1970, p. 521). On Super Sundays after 1994, artist Robert Markey installed a "scoreboard" in New York's Grand Central Station that showed the teams' scores together with the number of women battered in the United States since the opening kickoff: one woman every fifteen seconds (Cheng 1996). Here the issue of whether in fact domestic violence increases after the Super Bowl need not be addressed; the point is that even the "average" rate is shocking. This piece makes the association between football and violence, but equally important is its publicness, a large scoreboard in Grand Central Station no less, displaying the issue of domestic violence, previously something not openly discussed, as openly and publicly as the Super Bowl score.

Common Knowledge and History

Historical precedent is another way to generate common knowledge: for example, "if we were cut off on the telephone and you happened to call back as I waited, then if we are cut off again in the same call, I will wait again" (Lewis

1969, p. 36). This is nicely illustrated in how the employees of the Beverly Hills Supper Club helped customers evacuate during the May 28, 1977, fire: "Employees made certain that their rooms or their parties exited to safety, and seemed to assume a responsibility for those customers they were serving, but not necessarily for customers in other parts of the building." This fire, one of the worst in U.S. history, claimed 164 lives; in his analysis Richard L. Best (1977, p. 73) emphasizes that there was no prediscussed evacuation plan that "assigned specific responsibilities to employees." That waiters and waitresses only helped their "own" customers does not necessarily indicate callousness; without an explicitly communicated plan, the only way waiters and waitresses could coordinate was by established precedent (see also Canter 1980).

High-concept movies require not only intensive advertising, but also a "presold property": *Jaws* was based on a best-selling novel, and films such as *Dick Tracy*, *Superman*, and *The Addams Family* have been based on sometimes very old comic strips and television series. One interpretation of this is that because high-concept movies have very high production and marketing costs, studios try to use ideas that have a proven profit-generating record (Wyatt 1994, p. 78). But whatever blockbuster profits Dick Tracy, Superman, and the Addams Family enjoyed occurred decades before their movie adaptations, if ever. These characters are common knowledge not because of a recent mass success but because they are historical, appearing to small unexcited audiences but recurringly, year after year in comic strips and late-night syndicated television. In terms of common knowledge, history is just like publicity: when I see ads for *Independence Day* I know that everyone else knows something about it because I see the massive ad campaign; when I see ads for *The Addams Family* I know that everyone else knows something about it, because everyone knows about the Addams Family.

Thomas Schelling ([1960] 1980) noted that coordination problems can be solved by "focal points." The classic example is two people who want to meet each other somewhere in New York City when the time has been prearranged but the location has not. Both people only care about meeting each other, not the location, and there are as many possible coordinations as there are locations in the city. Facing this hypothetical problem, however, people typically choose the Empire State Building, Grand Central Station, and so on. In other words, shared ideas about what is "obvious" can help coordination even without any explicit communication. A recent example is how the 1989 demonstrations in Leipzig, which eventually took down the government of East Germany, were coordinated. Beginning in 1982, the Nikolai Church in downtown Leipzig held peace prayers every Monday afternoon, from five to six o'clock. "By mid-1989 the church and the peace prayers were firmly established in the minds of the people as an 'institution' of protest associated with the local oppositional subculture. It was commonly known that each Monday at about 6 P.M. a large number of people would come streaming out of both the Nikolai Church and other nearby churches that held late afternoon services. . . . [S]mall groups of friends typically met on Monday afternoons in the city center, where they would join churchgoers and other strangers to form a demonstration" (Lohmann 1994, p. 67). For many years, attendance in these demonstrations was relatively small (fewer than 1,000 people) but their regularity and long history enabled in October 1989 demonstrations of as many as 325,000 people, coming together spontaneously on Monday afternoons (Opp and Gern 1993, Lohmann 1994).

As we have seen, mechanisms of publicity are strategic resources in fights over how to coordinate. Thus we might expect that histories are also. French revolutionaries trying to free themselves of existing coordinations might try to efface recent history by appealing to a "mythic present" or trump it by appealing to the even older ideals of ancient Greece (Hunt 1984, p. 27). Scott (1990, p. 101) notes that the rhetoric of rebellion often appeals to existing conservative institutions, such as the church and king: "in France and Italy in the sixteenth and seventeenth centuries it was common for insurgent rioters to cry, 'Long Live the Virgin' (Viva Maria) and follow this with particular demands." Scott emphasizes that this should be understood not as evidence of "false consciousness" but as a strategic ploy: "it allows the king to grant the petition while appearing to enhance his prestige, and it offers a welcome defensive posture that may help limit damage if the initiative fails." Here we notice an additional strategic element: by "invoking the ritual symbols of a conservative hegemony," revolutionaries better create common knowledge: a person who hears their demands knows that everyone else can understand at least some aspect of it.

If history can help create common knowledge, then perhaps common knowledge can create history. What a society considers its history is not just the sum of its members' past experiences; the recording, interpreting, and collective "re-remembering" of past events take place in social institutions. Paul Connerton (1989, pp. 39–40) argues that "to study the social formation of memory is to study those acts of transfer that make remembering in common possible. . . . [I]mages of the past and recollected knowledge of the past are conveyed and sustained by (more or less ritual) performances," especially "commemorative ceremonies." Eric Hobsbawm (1983, pp. 304–5) finds a flurry of "invented traditions" between 1870 and 1914, as the advent of universal male suffrage made nations appeal to mass "audiences" for legitimacy, and relates this to the "invention in this period of substantially new constructions for spectacle and de facto mass ritual such as sports stadia, outdoor and indoor." The Kennedy assassination is often considered to be one of the central historical events of postwar U.S. history; perhaps this is partly because "it is probably the nearest equivalent in a large modern nation-state to the kind of intense mutual rededication ceremony that is possible in a smaller and simpler society" (Verba 1965, p. 354). According to Sidney Verba (1965, p. 355), "it may not be the event itself that is most significant for this ceremonial aspect. . . . [T]he fact that the reaction to the event was shared seems more important. It was in many cases shared by families gathered around television sets, it was shared in church services and other community ceremonials, but it was intensely and widely shared through the media themselves. Not only were the emotions of individual Americans involved, but they were made clearly aware of the emotions of their fellow Americans." Finally, the 1969 riot at the Stonewall Bar in New York City is widely understood as the pivotal event in the gay and lesbian rights movement, but, according to one participant, what made it a part of history was not so much the riot itself but its commemoration one year later: "if people hadn't decided to commemorate Stonewall with a political march, no one would remember Stonewall" (*After Stonewall* 1999).

Common Knowledge and Group Identity

People often coordinate in fairly arbitrary groups: I might enlist in the army and help protect your family in Miami because you agree to help protect mine in Chicago, but why don't I make this agreement with people in Toronto or Havana? Social linkages alone cannot be the reason; as Benedict Anderson (1991, p. 6) notes, "members of even the smallest nation will never know most of their fellow-members, meet them, or even hear of them." Yet nations are no doubt serious collective actors.

Anderson (1991, pp. 6, 44) defines a nation as an "imagined political community," where the meaning of "imagined" is essentially common knowledge: "Speakers of the huge variety of Frenches, Englishes, or Spanishes, who might find it difficult or even impossible to understand one another in conversation, became capable of comprehending one another via print and paper. In the process, they gradually became aware of the hundreds of thousands, even millions, of people in their particular language-field. . . . These fellow-readers . . . formed . . . the embryo of the nationally imagined community." Anderson (1991, pp. 35–36) calls reading the morning newspaper a "mass ceremony . . . performed in

silent privacy. . . . [E]ach communicant is well aware that
the ceremony he performs is being replicated simultaneously
by thousands (or millions) of others . . . [as he observes] exact replicas of his own paper being consumed by his subway,
barbershop, or residential neighbors." Here content, what
exactly these fellow readers are reading, does not matter
much; what matters is that each reader knows that other
readers are reading the same thing. Of course, this reasoning
applies not only to nations: on pilgrimage to Mecca, "the
Berber encountering the Malay before the Kaaba must, as it
were, ask himself: 'Why is this man doing what I am doing,
uttering the same words that I am uttering, even though we
can not talk to one another?' There is only one answer, once
one has learnt it: 'Because *we* are Muslims'" (Anderson
1991, p. 54). Perhaps it is not just the obviousness of the
commonality but the mutual obviousness: as we pray together, I discover that you know the same prayer as I do, I
know that you know that I know, and so on.

As Clark and Marshall (1992, p. 36) point out, belonging
to the same community is one way to form common knowledge: "the basic idea is that there are things *everyone* in a
community knows and assumes that everyone else in that
community knows, too." But we can also say that common
knowledge can to some degree generate community. Joseph
Turow (1997, p. 2) argues that the overall trend in advertising since the 1970s has been from mass marketing toward
niche marketing, due to innovations in more "targetable"
media (e.g., cable television, the internet, and specialized
magazines) as well as the development of the data gathering
and statistical methods required for successful targeting. The
consequence of this is social fragmentation, "the electronic
equivalents of gated communities."

The idea that group identities are formed through communication is not new. Nancy Fraser (1990, p. 100) recom-
mends the use of pragmatic theories that "insist on the social
context and social practice of communication, and study a
plurality of historically changing discursive sites and practices . . . [and therefore] offer us the possibility of thinking

of social identities as complex, changing, and discursively constructed." Common knowledge might be a useful concept for such theories.

After coming into power in South Africa in 1994, the African National Congress followed a deliberate policy of racial reconciliation; for example, ANC provincial premiers made a point to speak Afrikans (Waldmeir 1997, p. 269). The single most important symbolic action in this process was Nelson Mandela's appearance, in team uniform, on the playing field of the World Rugby Cup final in Johannesburg in May 1995. The seventy thousand stunned fans, predominantly white, started chanting "Nelson! Nelson!" and after the South African national team won, the entire nation erupted in celebration. Rugby, long a hated symbol of apartheid, was transformed in a single collective moment, a single common knowledge event, into something all South Africans could be proud about. According to Archbishop Desmond Tutu, it "was a defining moment in the life of our country. . . . Unbelievable that when we won, people could be dancing in Soweto. It had the effect of just turning around, I think, our country. It said it is actually possible for us to become one nation" (*The Long Walk of Nelson Mandela* 1999).

4

Conclusion

The distinction between rationality and irrationality in the Western tradition goes back at least to Aristotle (1976, p. 90), who wrote that the "irrational part of the soul" is persuaded and admonished by the rational part "in the sense that a child pays attention to its father." It is all too easy to say that this distinction is misleading or at the very least simplistic. For example, there seems to be a neurological connection between emotion and decision making in human beings; this is suggested by the phenomenon of people who, as a result of prefrontal brain damage, become both emotionally unresponsive and bad at making everyday decisions, even though their "pure reasoning" abilities, as measured by standard intelligence tests, for example, are undiminished (Damasio 1994).

Compared with the great complexity and richness of individual and social life, simple distinctions are by definition crude. But the standard argument is that to understand the social world in any generality, if one has ambitions other than chronicling infinite detail, one must use simple and crude concepts; for example, this book employs a very simple conception of individual thought and action and applies it widely. Theories and explanations can thus be much more clearly demarcated than reality itself. For example, although few would say that there is a clear distinction between the "rational part" and the "irrational part" of a human being, it seems obvious that there is a distinction between explanations based on rationality and explanations based on irrationality or nonrationality; Vilfredo Pareto institutionalized this distinction, calling it the dividing line between economics and sociology (see Swedberg 1990, p. 11).

This distinction, related to a whole series of distinctions, such as reason-culture, thinking-feeling, calculation-emotion and so on, is easily found in recent scholarship. For example, Jean Cohen (1985, p. 687), in an article on collective action dichotomously entitled "Strategy or Identity," distinguishes between the "resource-mobilization paradigm" and the "identity-oriented paradigm": "One cannot . . . simply add a consideration of solidarity, collective identity, consciousness, or ideology to the resource-mobilization perspective without bursting its framework. Clearly, the resource-mobilization perspective . . . operates with a concept of rational action that is too narrow and hence unable to address these questions." James Carey (1988, pp. 15, 18–20) writes that the "transmission view of communication . . . defined by terms such as 'imparting,' 'sending,' 'transmitting,' or 'giving information to others'" has in American scholarship dominated the "ritual view of communication . . . linked to terms such as 'sharing,' 'participation,' 'association,' 'fellowship,' and 'the possession of a common faith.'" This is because of "our obsessive individualism, which makes psychological life the paramount reality . . . [and] our Puritanism, which leads to disdain for the significance of human activity that is not practical."

This book tries to show that this distinction cannot be so easily maintained. It starts with a narrow, unadorned conception of rationality in the context of coordination problems and shows that the common knowledge required is substantially related to issues of intersubjectivity, collective consciousness, and group identity. It starts with isolated individuals facing real, practical problems of coordination and shows that transcending the "transmission" view of communication (first-order knowledge) and including the "ritual" view (common knowledge) is exactly what is required.

The material-cultural distinction is located by William Sewell (1993, p. 25) in Christian metaphysics' distinction between base and spirit, and he argues against it on the grounds of reality: for example, the economic world of production and exchange is not solely material because money, pieces of paper with pictures on them, is essentially symbolic; the world of ideas is not solely cultural because it involves "the manipulation of physical substances—paper, ink, or computer keyboards; vibrating columns of air, lecterns, pulpits, or soapboxes; lecture halls, churches, studies, or libraries." This book argues against this distinction also, but not on the grounds of actual human experience, which is of course valid. The argument here is based on the logic of rationality itself. That is, even narrowly rational *Homo economicus* when solving coordination problems must form common knowledge, which we understand here as an aspect of rituals.

The idea that rational choice theory, in particular game theory, might be helpful in looking at cultural practices might seem novel, but was in fact advocated more than thirty years ago by Erving Goffman (1969) in, among other books, *Strategic Interaction,* and Claude Lévi-Strauss (1963, p. 298), who explicitly stated that game theory allowed the "increasing consolidation of social anthropology, economics, and linguistics into one great field, that of communication." The explicit application of game theory to symbolic action and culture, presaged by the work of Schelling ([1960] 1980), has recently been pursued in several directions (notably O'Neill 2000 and Schuessler 2000; see also Bates and Weingast 1995, Lichbach and Zuckerman 1997, and Bermeo 1997 for discussion). I argue that this development should not be considered a diversion or side application but rather a necessary step in game theory's own internal agenda. The argument is not that cultural practices are additional side topics that it would be nice for rational choice theory to look into. The argument is that the agenda of rational choice theory itself demands it.

Game theory is often used simply because it can make some kind of prediction when other kinds of reasoning do not. The textbook example in economics, for instance, is that of oligopoly. When there is a monopoly (a single firm), a prediction can be made by assuming profit maximization; when there is a competitive market (numerous firms, each too small to influence the equilibrium price), a prediction can be made by assuming that supply equals demand. In oligopoly, in which several firms interdependently influence prices, game theory is called upon to find an equilibrium, to make a prediction.

Sometimes, however, game theory is simply not good at prediction. Many game theoretic models have a large number of equilibria. For example, take the case of whether people drive on the right side of the road or on the left. Everyone driving on the right is an equilibrium in the sense that given that everyone else drives on the right, no one wants to "deviate" and drive on the left. Everyone driving on the left is also an equilibrium. Here there are two equilibria; we might be able to predict that everyone will drive on the same side, but we cannot predict whether that side will be the left or right. This is a very simple example, but, in general, the problem of indeterminacy can be severe, with many equilibria possible.

There are several ways of responding to this problem, which is a fundamental one. One is to try to squeeze as much predictive power as possible from the game itself, assuming that the objective is to make a unique prediction in any game and developing axioms that allow one to do so (as exemplified by Harsanyi and Selten 1988). Another is to consider explicitly the social process, external to the game, by which people coordinate on an equilibrium. Broadly speaking, there are at least three kinds of models that do this.

Much recent work in game theory models individuals in a game as learning, adapting, or being selected in an evolutionary process (e.g., Samuelson 1998, Young 1998). The idea is that some equilibria might be more likely than others to result from a dynamic process of adaptation. This approach, which typically assumes that people follow simple learning rules or adaptations, is also often intended to counter the common objection that game theory assumes hyperrationality. The second approach is focal points, as discussed earlier, which are often interpreted as an aspect of a society's culture; for example, New Yorkers are more likely to choose

Grand Central Station as a place to meet while non–New Yorkers are more likely to choose the Empire State Building; the "focalness" of Grand Central Station can be understood as part of New York local culture.

Both of these approaches are important, but assume that the coordination process is not purposeful. The adaptive or evolutionary approach is reminiscent of "invisible hand" explanations in that people do not purposefully coordinate; coordination "just happens" without anyone planning or even thinking about it. Focal points are usually understood as something given exogenously (e.g., Kreps 1990), despite Schelling's ([1960] 1980, p. 144; see also Calvert 1992) observation that "when there is no apparent focal point for agreement, [a person] can create one by his power to make a dramatic suggestion." The third approach, which we employ in this book, is to consider coordination as an active, purposeful process achieved through explicit communication (see Johnson 1993). Coordination is often achieved through adaptation and evolution, and implicit communication, but often people explicitly communicate. If we observe two people enjoying each other's company at a restaurant, it is possible that one of them "mutated" and just happened to walk in, and the other one adapted by following her in, and it is also possible that they met there by some implicit agreement, but it is safest to assume that they simply made a date. Of course, this communication process is much more complicated for more than two people, but this is what this book is about.

If we look at how people explicitly communicate in order to solve coordination problems, the issue of common knowledge immediately arises, from standard game theoretic reasoning as well as linguistic theories of meaning and strong commonsense intuitions. Looking at how common knowledge is formed in societies, one is necessarily drawn to communicative events that look like rituals: ceremonies, media events, and so forth. By associating common knowledge with cultural practices, this book suggests a close and reciprocal relationship between the perspectives of rationality and culture, which are often thought separate or even antagonistic. The idea of individual rationality, historically associated with atomistic market societies, can help in understanding cultural practices which seem to create social unity. The study of culture has long considered economic contexts; pursuing the logical consequences of "material" rationality, game theory finds culture.

Appendix

The Argument Expressed Diagrammatically

Modeling Coordination Problems

In our example of two co-workers on the bus, each person wants to get off the bus and get a drink only if the other person gets off also. A person's motivations can be represented by assigning to each outcome a number that corresponds to its payoff or utility. For example, the worst thing for me would be if I got off and you stayed on, because I would feel bad about having a drink without you being there; this would give me a payoff of 0. The best thing for me would be if we both got off; we would enjoy a drink together and this would give me a payoff of 6. If I stay on the bus, I get the "status quo" utility of 4, regardless of whether you get off or not.

	You get off	You stay on
I get off	6	0
I stay on	4	4
	My payoff	

Assuming that you and I are similar, we can write down your utilities: the worst thing for you is if you get off and I stay on, and so forth.

	You get off	You stay on
I get off	6	4
I stay on	0	4
	Your payoff	

Instead of two tables, it is convenient to write them together in a single table. For each outcome, there is a pair of
numbers: my payoff and then your payoff.

	You get off	You stay on
I get off	6, 6	0, 4
I stay on	4, 0	4, 4

My payoff, your payoff

By inspecting the table, one can see that I want to get off
only if you get off, and you want to get off only if I get off.
The power and crudity of game theory is that the great variety of coordination problems can all be represented by a
table like this one.

Modeling Metaknowledge

Common knowledge and metaknowledge generally were
given a mathematical formalization by Robert Aumann (1976)
(an equivalent representation is an "interactive belief system" as in O'Neill 2000). First list every possible state of the
world: on the bus, when our mutual acquaintance yells, say
that I am either awake or asleep, and you are either awake
or asleep. Hence there are four possible states of the world:
"I'm awake, you're awake," "I'm awake, you're asleep,"
"I'm asleep, you're awake," and "I'm asleep, you're asleep."
    Each person has a different ability to distinguish what the
real state of the world is. For example, take the case in
which we face each other: I am looking at you, and you are
looking at me (Figure 16).
    When I am asleep, I cannot tell whether you are asleep or
not, but when I'm awake, I can. We can represent this by
drawing the following ovals, which partition the set of states
of the world (Figure 17).
    The idea here is that when two states of the world are in

Figure 16. Facing each other.

the same oval, I cannot tell these two states apart; when two
states of the world are in different ovals, I can tell them
apart. Because "I'm asleep, you're awake" and "I'm asleep,
you're asleep" are in the same oval, this means that I cannot
distinguish between these two states. Similarly, when you are
awake, you can tell if I am awake; your knowledge is represented by the ovals in Figure 18.

What is it that people know? People know events, where
an event is simply a set of states of the world. For example,
Figure 19 presents three events, diagrammed as "boxes":
you're awake, we're both awake, and one of us is awake.
Take, for example, the event that you're awake. If we write
this down along with my ovals, we get Figure 20. Here the
box represents the event that you are awake. Notice that
the oval surrounding "I'm awake, you're awake" stays inside
the box. When I'm awake and you're awake, I know that the
state is in this oval; because the oval is contained in the box,
I know that you are awake. However, notice that the oval
surrounding "I'm asleep, you're awake" goes outside the
box. When I'm asleep and you're awake, I cannot tell this
state apart from "I'm asleep, you're asleep"; since the oval
goes outside the box, I cannot know for sure that you are
awake.

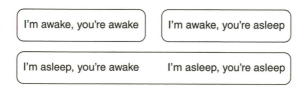

Figure 17. My ovals.

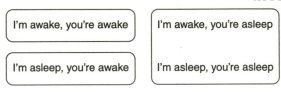

Figure 18. Your ovals.

So, as indicated by the ovals, I only know you're awake
when we are both awake. But we can think of "I know you
are awake" as just another event, as shown in Figure 21.
This is simply the same event as the event that we're both
awake. Now we can take this event to your ovals, as shown
in Figure 22.

Again, if your oval stays inside the box, you know that the
event has happened. Here, the event is me knowing you're
awake. When we're both awake, at state "You're awake, I'm

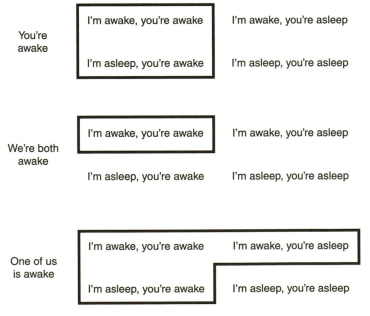

Figure 19. Various events.

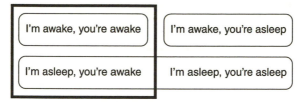

Figure 20. When I'm awake and you're awake, I know you're awake; when I'm asleep and you're awake, I don't.

awake," your oval stays inside the box; hence you know the event that I know you're awake; that is, you know that I know that you're awake.

Further levels of metaknowledge just involve doing this process iteratively; one can see that in this example, when we're both awake, I know that you know that . . . you're awake holds for arbitrarily many levels. Hence we can say that when we're both awake, it is common knowledge that you're awake.

To see how something can be known to everyone but not common knowledge, consider the case in Figure 23 in which you are facing away from me, so that I can see you but you cannot see me. My ovals are the same as before: when I'm awake, I can tell if you are asleep or not (I can see your head nodding over). But your ovals are different: now even when you are awake, you cannot tell whether I am awake or not, since you cannot see me. Hence your new ovals (dotted for contrast) are shown in Figure 24.

My ovals have not changed, and hence again the event that I know that you're awake is the event that we are both

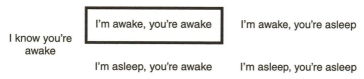

Figure 21. The event that I know you're awake.

Figure 22. When I'm awake and you're awake, you know that I know you're awake.

awake. When we take this event to your new ovals, however, we get Figure 25.

Now, at the state "I'm awake, you're awake," your oval goes outside the box: you do not know that I know that you are awake. When we are both awake, I know that you are awake, and you know that you are awake. But you do not know that I know that you are awake. When we are both awake, we both know that you are awake, but it is not common knowledge.

Why Common Knowledge Is Good for Solving Coordination Problems

So far the coordination problem has been represented as tables of numbers, and your knowledge and my knowledge have been represented as ovals. The tables of numbers, our payoffs, describe our preferences about getting off the bus. The ovals describe the communication process: if we face each other, then you have different ovals than if you are facing away, for example. To describe fully the communication process, we specify two more things. First, we specify what

Figure 23. You face away.

Figure 24. Your ovals in the case in which you face away.

happens when a person does not receive the message: here a sleeping person does not hear the yell and hence we assume that a sleeping person stays on the bus, the "status quo" action. Second, we specify how likely each state of the world is: here we assume that each person is just as likely to be awake as asleep, and therefore each of the four states of the world is equally likely.

Now that we have completely specified both our payoffs and the communication process, we can figure out what you and I will do. Consider the case in which we face each other. All we have to do is fill out the diagram in Figure 26. This diagram specifies what each of us will do in each state of the world. Notice our assumption that a sleeping person stays on the bus.

Say that we're at state "I'm awake, you're asleep"; what would I choose to do? I can see from Figure 26 that you stay on the bus. Hence, I look at my payoff table: if I get off the bus, I get a payoff of 0; if I stay on the bus, I get a payoff of 4. So I choose to stay on the bus. Similarly, at state "I'm asleep, you're awake," you decide to stay on the bus since you see me sleeping (Figure 27).

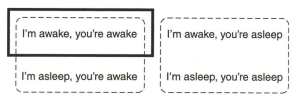

Figure 25. You do not know that I know that you are awake.

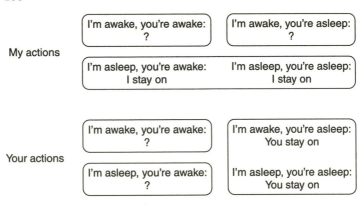

Figure 26. Our actions in each state of the world.

What happens at state "I'm awake, you're awake"? If one of us got off and the other stayed on, the situation would be "unstable" because one of us would want to change her action. Hence the two possibilities are that either we both get off or we both stay on, as shown in Figures 28 and 29. Both of these situations are "equilibria" in that neither person, given the other person's actions, would choose to do something different. In the "successful" equilibrium, when we are both awake, you get off, and hence it is my interest to get off

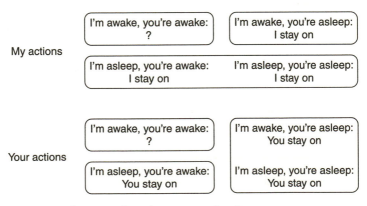

Figure 27. If you see the other person sleeping, you stay on.

Figure 28. The "successful" equilibrium.

also (I get a payoff of 6 instead of 4). Similarly, when we are both awake, given that I get off, you want to get off also. In the "unsuccessful" equilibrium, when we are both awake, I stay on because you stay on (I get a payoff of 4 instead of 0), and you stay on because I stay on. In the successful equilibrium, we manage to get off the bus as a result of the yell. In the unsuccessful equilibrium, we never get off the bus.

Now consider the case in which you face away from me

Figure 29. The "unsuccessful" equilibrium.

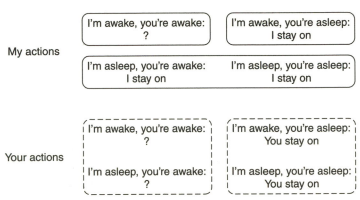

Figure 30. Our actions in the case in which you face away.

(Figure 30). As discussed earlier, because you are facing away from me, your ovals are different: now even when you are awake, you can't tell if I am awake or not. Again, we assume that a sleeping person stays on the bus. Also, at state "I'm awake, you're asleep," again I choose to stay on the bus because I see you sleeping.

What will you do at states "I'm awake, you're awake" and "I'm asleep, you're awake"? First, because you cannot distinguish between these states (they're in the same oval) you have to choose the same action in both. In other words, because you cannot tell if I am awake or not, you cannot condition your action on whether I am awake or not. All you know is that I am awake with probability 1/2 and asleep with probability 1/2 (from our assumption that each state is equally likely). If you stay on the bus, then you get a payoff of 4 regardless of what I do. If you get off, then with probability 1/2, I am asleep and you get a payoff of 0; with probability 1/2, I am awake and either I get off also and you get a payoff of 6, or I stay on the bus and you get a payoff of 0. So by getting off, you get at best 0 with probability 1/2 and 6 with probability 1/2; this "lottery" is roughly equivalent to getting a payoff of 3. Because this is lower than the payoff of 4 you get by staying on, you decide to stay on. In other

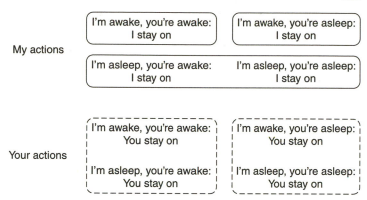

My actions

I'm awake, you're awake: | I'm awake, you're asleep:
I stay on | I stay on

I'm asleep, you're awake: | I'm asleep, you're asleep:
I stay on | I stay on

Your actions

I'm awake, you're awake: | I'm awake, you're asleep:
You stay on | You stay on

I'm asleep, you're awake: | I'm asleep, you're asleep:
You stay on | You stay on

Figure 31. The only equilibrium in the case in which you face away.

words, knowing that I get off with a probability of at most 1/2 is not enough to make you want to get off too. So at states "I'm awake, you're awake" and "I'm asleep, you're awake," you do not get off the bus. Hence at state "I'm awake, you're awake," I do not get off the bus either. Hence we have Figure 31.

So in no state of the world do we manage to coordinate and get off the bus. This is the only equilibrium in the case in which you face away. At state "I'm awake, you're awake," even though we are both awake and both hear the yell, you do not get off because you cannot tell if I'm awake; hence even though I know you are awake and hear the yell, I do not get off. At state "I'm awake, you're awake," we both know about the yell but it is not common knowledge.

When we face each other, when we are both awake, that fact is common knowledge, and successful coordination, although not guaranteed (there is also the "unsuccessful" equilibrium), is at least possible. When you are facing away, successful coordination is not possible, even when both of us get the message.

References _____

After Stonewall. 1999. Film produced by John Scagliotti, Vic Basile, Janet Baus, and Dan Hunt. First Run Features, New York.

Amos, Denise. 1991. "Super Bowl Advertising Game Plan: Keep It Simple." *St. Petersburg Times*, January 25, p. 1E.

Anderson, Benedict. 1991. *Imagined Communities: Reflections on the Origin and Spread of Nationalism.* Rev. ed. London: Verso.

Aristotle. 1976. *The Ethics of Aristotle: The Nicomachean Ethics.* Translated by J.A.K. Thomson. Revised edition translated by Hugh Tredennick. London: Penguin.

Auerbach, Jon, and Beppi Crosariol. 1995. "Microsoft's Blockbuster: Backed by a $200 Million Blitz, Windows 95 Is Coming to a PC Screen near You." *Boston Globe*, August 20, p. 89.

Aumann, Robert J. 1974. "Subjectivity and Correlation in Randomized Strategies." *Journal of Mathematical Economics* 1: 67–96.

———. 1976. "Agreeing to Disagree." *Annals of Statistics* 4: 1236–39.

Austin, John. 1975. *How to Do Things with Words.* 2d ed. Edited by J. O. Urmson and Marina Sbisa. Cambridge, Mass.: Harvard University Press.

Baron-Cohen, Simon. 1995. *Mindblindness: An Essay on Autism and Theory of the Mind.* Cambridge, Mass.: MIT Press.

Baron-Cohen, Simon, Helen Tager-Flusberg, and Donald J. Cohen. 2000. *Understanding Other Minds: Perspectives from Developmental Cognitive Neuroscience.* 2d ed. Oxford: Oxford University Press.

Bates, Robert H., and Barry R. Weingast. 1995. "A New Comparative Politics: Integrating Rational Choice and Interpretivist Perspectives." Paper presented at the American Political Science Association Meetings, Chicago, August 1995.

Becker, Gary S. 1991. "A Note on Restaurant Pricing and Other Examples of Social Influences on Price." *Journal of Political Economy* 99: 1109–16.

Becker, Gary S., and Kevin M. Murphy. 1993. "A Simple Theory of Advertising as a Good or Bad." *Quarterly Journal of Economics* 108: 941–64.

Bentham, Jeremy. 1791 [1843]. *Panopticon; or, The Inspection-House; Containing the Idea of a New Principle of Construction Applicable to Any Sort of Establishment, in which Persons of Any Description Are To Be Kept Under Inspection; and in Particular to Penitentiary-Houses, Prisons, Poor-Houses, Lazarettos, Houses of Industry, Manufactories, Hospitals, Work-Houses, Mad-Houses, and Schools: With a Plan of Management Adapted to the Principle: In a Series of Letters, Written in the Year 1787, from Crecheff in White Russia, to a Friend in England.* In *The Works of Jeremy Bentham*, published under the superintendence of his executor, John Bowring. Vol. 4. Edinburgh: William Tait.

Berk, Richard A. 1974. "A Gaming Approach to Crowd Behavior." *American Sociological Review* 39: 355–73.

Bermeo, Nancy, ed. 1997. "Notes from the Annual Meetings: Culture and Rational Choice." *Newsletter of the APSA Organized Section in Comparative Politics* 8, no. 2: 5–21.

Best, Richard L. 1977. *Reconstruction of a Tragedy: The Beverly Hills Supper Club Fire.* Boston: National Fire Protection Association.

Biskind, Peter. 1975. "The Politics of Power in 'On the Waterfront.'" *Film Quarterly* 25, no. 1 (Fall): 25–38.

Bloch, Maurice. 1974. "Symbols, Song, Dance and Features of Articulation." *Archives Européenes de Sociologie* 15: 55–81.

Boorstin, Daniel J. 1961. *The Image: A Guide to Pseudo-Events in America.* New York: Harper & Row.

Brothers, Leslie. 1997. *Friday's Footprint: How Society Shapes the Human Mind.* New York: Oxford University Press.

Burke, David. 1997. "Legal Woes Give an Unhappy Twist to the Dream of a Young Boy Playing with His First Radio." *Decatur Herald and Review*, January 12, p. 4A.

Calvert, Randall L. 1992. "Leadership and Its Basis in Problems of Social Coordination." *International Political Science Review* 13: 7–24.

Canter, David. 1980. "Fires and Human Behavior—An Introduction." In *Fires and Human Behaviour*, edited by David Canter, pp. 1–12. Chichester: John Wiley and Sons.

Carey, James W. 1988. *Communication as Culture: Essays on Media and Society.* Boston: Unwin Hyman.

Chapkis, Wendy. 1986. *Beauty Secrets: Women and the Politics of Appearance.* Boston: South End Press.

Cheng, Mae M. 1996. "Keeping a More Horrifying Score: Game-Time Tally of Domestic Abuse." *Newsday*, January 28, p. A6.

Chong, Dennis. 1991. *Collective Action and the Civil Rights Movement*. Chicago: University of Chicago Press.

Chwe, Michael Suk-Young. 1998. "Culture, Circles, and Commercials: Publicity, Common Knowledge, and Social Coordination." *Rationality and Society* 10: 47–75.

———. 1999a. "The Reeded Edge and the Phillips Curve: Money Neutrality, Common Knowledge, and Subjective Beliefs." *Journal of Economic Theory* 87: 49–71.

———. 1999b. "Structure and Strategy in Collective Action." *American Journal of Sociology* 105: 128–56.

———. 2000. "Communication and Coordination in Social Networks." *Review of Economic Studies* 67: 1–16.

Clark, Herbert H., and Catherine R. Marshall. 1992. "Definite Reference and Mutual Knowledge." In *Arenas of Language Use*, edited by Herbert H. Clark, pp. 9–59. Chicago: University of Chicago Press.

Cohen, Abner. 1974. *Two-Dimensional Man: An Essay on the Anthropology of Power and Symbolism in Complex Society*. Berkeley: University of California Press.

Cohen, Jean. 1985. "Strategy or Identity: New Theoretical Paradigms and Contemporary Social Movements." *Social Research* 52: 663–716.

Cohen, Jeff, and Norman Solomon. 1993. "Closing Eyes and Ears to Domestic Violence." *Cleveland Plain Dealer*, February 13, p. 4B.

Coleman, James S. 1988. "Social Capital in the Creation of Human Capital." *American Journal of Sociology* 94 (suppl.): S95–S120.

Connerton, Paul. 1989. *How Societies Remember*. Cambridge: Cambridge University Press.

Coser, Lewis A. 1990. "The Intellectuals in Soviet Reform: On 'Pluralistic Ignorance' and Mass Communications." *Dissent* 37 (Spring): 181–83.

Cowen, Tyler. 2000. *What Price Fame?* Cambridge, Mass.: Harvard University Press.

Curtis, Russell L., and Benigno E. Aguirre. 1993. *Collective Behavior and Social Movements*. Boston: Allyn and Bacon.

d'Aquili, Eugene G., and Charles D. Laughlin Jr. 1979. "The Neurobiology of Myth and Ritual." In *The Spectrum of Ritual: A Biogenetic Structural Analysis*, edited by Eugene G. d'Aquili, Charles D. Laughlin Jr., and John McManus, pp. 152–82. New York: Columbia University Press.

Damasio, Antonio R. 1994. *Descartes' Error: Emotion, Reason, and the Human Brain*. New York: Avon Books.

Davison, W. Phillips. 1983. "The Third-Person Effect in Communication." *Public Opinion Quarterly* 47: 1–15.

Dayan, Daniel, and Elihu Katz. 1992. *Media Events: The Live Broadcasting of History*. Cambridge, Mass.: Harvard University Press.

Debord, Guy. [1967] 1995. *The Society of the Spectacle*. Translated by Donald Nicholson-Smith. Cambridge, Mass.: MIT Press. Originally published as *La Société du Spectacle* (Paris: Buchet-Chastel, 1967).

De Vany, Arthur, and David W. Walls. 1999. "Uncertainty in the Movie Industry: Does Star Power Reduce the Terror of the Box Office?" *Journal of Cultural Economics* 23: 285–318.

Diehl, Jackson. 1992. "Israeli Army's New 'Open Fire' Orders against Palestinians Draw Criticism." *Washington Post*, May 7, p. A37.

Dixit, Avinash, and Victor Norman. 1978. "Advertising and Welfare." *Bell Journal of Economics* 9: 1–17.

Durkheim, Emile. 1912 [1995]. *The Elementary Forms of Religious Life*. Translated by Karen E. Fields. New York: Free Press.

Erickson, Gladys A. 1957. *Warden Ragen of Joliet*. New York: E. P. Dutton.

Fernandez, Roberto M., and Doug McAdam. 1988. "Social Networks and Social Movements: Multiorganizational Fields and Recruitment to Freedom Summer." *Sociological Forum* 3: 357–82.

Fisher, Franklin M., John J. McGowan, and David S. Evans. 1980. "The Audience-Revenue Relationship for Local Television Stations." *Bell Journal of Economics* 11: 694–708.

Foucault, Michel. 1979. *Discipline and Punish: The Birth of the Prison*. Translated by Alan Sheridan. New York: Vintage.

Fournier, Gary M., and Donald L. Martin. 1983. "Does Government-Restricted Entry Produce Market Power? New Evidence from the Market for Television Advertising." *Bell Journal of Economics* 14: 44–56.

Fraser, Nancy. 1989. *Unruly Practices: Power, Discourse, and Gender in Contemporary Social Theory*. Minneapolis: University of Minnesota Press.

———. 1990. "The Uses and Abuses of French Discourse Theories for Feminist Politics." *boundary 2* 17: 82–101.

Fried, Michael. 1967. "Art and Objecthood." *Art Forum* 5, no. 10 (June 1967): 12–23.

Geanakoplos, John. 1992. "Common Knowledge." *Journal of Economic Perspectives* 6: 53–82.

Geertz, Clifford. 1973. *The Interpretation of Cultures: Selected Essays by Clifford Geertz.* New York: Basic Books.

———. 1980. *Negara: The Theatre State in Nineteenth-Century Bali.* Princeton: Princeton University Press.

———. 1983. "Centers, Kings, and Charisma: Reflections on the Symbolics of Power." In *Local Knowledge: Further Essays in Interpretive Anthropology,* pp. 121–46. New York: Basic Books.

Gilboa, Itzhak. 1998. *Theoretical Aspects of Rationality and Knowledge: Proceedings of the Seventh Conference (TARK 1998): July 22–24, 1998, Evanston, Illinois, USA.* San Francisco: Morgan Kaufmann.

Goffman, Erving. 1969. *Strategic Interaction.* Philadelphia: University of Pennsylvania Press.

Goodsell, Charles T. 1988. *The Social Meaning of Civic Space: Studying Political Authority through Architecture.* Lawrence: University Press of Kansas.

Gorov, Lynda. 1993. "Activists: Abused Women at Risk on Super Sunday." *Boston Globe,* January 29, p. 13.

Gould, Roger V. 1993. "Collective Action and Network Structure." *American Sociological Review* 58: 182–96.

———. 1995. *Insurgent Identities: Class, Community, and Protest in Paris from 1848 to the Commune.* Chicago: University of Chicago Press.

Granovetter, Mark. 1973. "The Strength of Weak Ties." *American Journal of Sociology* 78: 1360–80.

———. 1995. *Getting a Job: A Study of Contacts and Careers.* 2d ed. Chicago: University of Chicago Press.

Griffiths, Paul. 1995. "Gambling for Life: The Met Unveils a New Production of Tchaikovsky's 'Queen of Spades.'" *New Yorker,* November 20, pp. 121–23.

Habermas, Jürgen. 1977 [1986]. "Hannah Arendt's Communications Concept of Power." In *Power,* edited by Steven Lukes, pp. 75–93. New York: New York University Press. Originally published in *Social Research* 44 (1977): 3–24.

———. 1989. *The Theory of Communicative Action.* Vol. 1. Boston: Beacon Press.

Hardin, Russell. 1995. *One for All: The Logic of Group Conflict.* Princeton: Princeton University Press.

Harsanyi, John C., and Reinhard Selten. 1988. *A General Theory of Equilibrium Selection in Games.* Cambridge, Mass.: MIT Press.

Harvey, Anna. 1999. "Partisanship as a Social Convention." Working paper, New York University.

Helm, Leslie. 1995. "Global Hype Raises the Curtain on Windows 95: Microsoft Introduces New Software—and Softer Image—with Myriad of Grandiose Gimmicks." *Los Angeles Times*, August 24, p. A1.

Hobsbawm, Eric. 1983. "Mass-Producing Traditions: Europe, 1870–1914." In *The Invention of Tradition*, edited by Eric Hobsbawm and Terence Ranger, pp. 263–307. Cambridge: Cambridge University Press.

Horovitz, Bruce. 1987. "Marketing: Super Bowl Is the Event in Ad Game." *Los Angeles Times*, January 6, pt. 4, p. 9.

Horton, William S., and Boaz Keysar. 1996. "When Do Speakers Take into Account Common Ground?" *Cognition* 59: 91–117.

Hunt, Lynn. 1984. *Politics, Culture, and Class in the French Revolution.* Berkeley: University of California Press.

Isaacson, Melissa. 1996. "NFL's Stance on Domestic Abuse Far Short of Super." *Chicago Tribune*, January 21, sports section, p. 3.

Jakobson, Roman. 1966. "Grammatical Parallelism and Its Russian Facet." *Language* 42: 399–429.

Jehl, Douglas. 1996. "Egypt Adding Corn to Bread: An Explosive Mix?" *New York Times*, November 27, p. A4.

Johnson, Bradley. 1994. "The Commercial, and the Product, which Changed Advertising." *Advertising Age*, January 10, pp. 1–14.

Johnson, James. 1993. "Is Talk Really Cheap? Prompting Conversation between Critical Theory and Rational Choice." *American Political Science Review* 87: 74–86.

Johnson, Norris. 1987. "Panic at 'The Who Concert Stampede': An Empirical Assessment." *Social Problems* 34: 362–73.

Julius, N. H. 1831. *Leçons sur les prisons.* Translated by H. Lagarmitte. Paris: F. G. Levrault.

Kahn, Joseph P. 1989. "Super Bowl III-D." *Boston Globe*, January 20, p. 27.

Katz, Michael L., and Carl Shapiro. 1994. "Systems Competition and Network Effects." *Journal of Economic Perspectives* 8: 93–115.

Keesing, Roger M. 1987. "Anthropology as an Interpretive Quest." *Current Anthropology* 28: 161–76.

Keller, Kevin Lane. 1993. "Conceptualizing, Measuring, and Managing Customer-Based Brand Equity." *Journal of Marketing* 57: 1–22.

Kelly, Kevin. 1997. "New Rules for the New Economy." *Wired* 5, no. 9 (September): 140–97.

Kihlstrom, Richard E., and Michael H. Riordan. 1984. "Advertising as a Signal." *Journal of Political Economy* 92: 427–50.

Kochen, Manfred. 1989. *The Small World*. Norwood, N.J.: Ablex.

Kreps, David M. 1990. "Corporate Culture and Economic Theory." In *Perspectives on Positive Political Economy*, edited by James E. Alt and Kenneth A. Shepsle, pp. 90–143. New York: Cambridge University Press.

Kuran, Timur. 1991. "Now Out of Never: The Element of Surprise in the East European Revolution of 1989." *World Politics* 44: 7–48.

———. 1995. *Private Truths, Public Lies: The Social Consequences of Preference Falsification*. Cambridge, Mass.: Harvard University Press.

Laitin, David D. 1986. *Hegemony and Culture: Politics and Religious Change among the Yoruba*. Chicago: University of Chicago Press.

———. 1994. "The Tower of Babel as a Coordination Game: Political Linguistics in Ghana." *American Political Science Review* 88: 622–34.

Lambert, Gerard B. 1956. *All Out of Step: A Personal Chronicle*. New York: Doubleday.

Lane, Randall. 1993. "Prepackaged Celebrity." *Forbes*, December 20, p. 86.

Lee, Namhee. 2000. "Minjung, History, and Subjectivity: The South Korean Student Movement and the Making of Minjung, 1960–1987." Ph.D. dissertation, University of Chicago.

Lekson, Stephen H. 1984. *Great Pueblo Architecture of Chaco Canyon, New Mexico*. Albuquerque, N.M.: National Park Service.

Lennen, Philip W. 1926. "In Memoriam: An Appreciation of Milton Feasley—A Real Advertising Man." *Printers' Ink* 137, no. 2 (October 14): 25–28.

Lev, Michael. 1991. "Super Bowl 25: The Football Hoopla Yields to Hype." *New York Times*, January 6, sec. 3, p. 5.

Lévi-Strauss, Claude. 1963. *Structural Anthropology.* Translated by Claire Jacobson and Brooke Grundfest Schoepf. New York: Basic Books.

Lewis, David K. 1969. *Convention: A Philosophical Study.* Cambridge, Mass.: Harvard University Press.

Lichbach, Mark Irving, and Alan S. Zuckerman, eds. 1997. *Comparative Politics: Rationality, Culture, and Structure.* New York: Cambridge University Press.

Lipe, William D., and Michelle Hegmon, eds. 1989. *The Architecture of Social Integration in Prehistoric Pueblos.* Cortez, Colo.: Crow Canyon Archaeological Center.

Lipsyte, Robert. 1993. "Super Bowl XXVII: Violence Translates at Home." *New York Times,* January 31, sec. 8, p. 5.

Lohmann, Susanne. 1994. "The Dynamics of Informational Cascades: The Monday Demonstrations in Leipzig, East Germany, 1989–91." *World Politics* 47: 42–101.

The Long Walk of Nelson Mandela. 1999. Television episode of *Frontline,* airing May 25, 1999. Produced by David Fanning and Indra deLanerolle. Directed by Clifford Bestall.

Luhmann, Niklas. 1985. *A Sociological Theory of Law.* Translated by Elizabeth King and Martin Albrow. London: Routledge and Kegan Paul.

Macy, Michael W. 1991. "Chains of Cooperation: Threshold Effects in Collective Action." *American Sociological Review* 56: 730–47.

Marchand, Roland. 1985. *Advertising the American Dream: Making Way for Modernity, 1920–1940.* Berkeley: University of California Press.

Marwell, Gerald, and Pamela Oliver. 1993. *The Critical Mass in Collective Action.* Cambridge: Cambridge University Press.

McAdam, Doug. 1986. "Recruitment to High-Risk Activism: The Case of Freedom Summer." *American Journal of Sociology* 92: 64–90.

McAdam, Doug, and Ronnelle Paulsen. 1993. "Specifying the Relationship between Social Ties and Activism." *American Journal of Sociology* 99: 640–67.

McCrone, John. 1994. "Don't Forget Your Memory Aide." *New Scientist,* February 5, p. 32–36.

McGraw, Dan. 1999. "Web Mania Hits Super Sunday." *USA Today,* February 8, p. 40.

McNaught, Brian. 1993. *Gay Issues in the Workplace.* New York: St. Martin's Press.

Milgram, Stanley. 1992. *The Individual in a Social World: Essays and Experiments.* Edited by John Sabini and Maury Silver. 2d ed. New York: McGraw-Hill.

Milgrom, Paul. 1981. "An Axiomatic Characterization of Common Knowledge." *Econometrica* 49: 219–22.

Milgrom, Paul, and John Roberts. 1986. "Price and Advertising Signals of Product Quality." *Journal of Political Economy* 94: 796–821.

Monderer, Dov, and Dov Samet. 1989. "Approximating Common Knowledge with Common Beliefs." *Games and Economic Behavior* 1: 170–90.

Montgomery, James D. 1991. "Social Networks and Labor-Market Outcomes: Toward an Economic Analysis." *American Economic Review* 81: 1408–18.

Moore, Will H. 1995. "Rational Rebels: Overcoming the Free-Rider Problem." *Political Research Quarterly* 48: 417–54.

Morgan, Robin, ed. 1970. *Sisterhood Is Powerful: An Anthology of Writings from the Women's Liberation Movement.* New York: Vintage.

Morris, Stephen. 1999. "Approximate Common Knowledge Revisited." *International Journal of Game Theory* 28: 385–408.

Morris, Stephen, Rafael Rob, and Hyun Song Shin. 1995. "p-Dominance and Belief Potential." *Econometrica* 63: 145–57.

Morris, Stephen, and Hyun Song Shin. 1999. "Private versus Public Information in Coordination Problems." Working paper, Yale University and Oxford University.

Mullen, Brian, and Li-tze Hu. 1988. "Social Projection as a Function of Cognitive Mechanisms: Two Meta-Analytic Integrations." *British Journal of Social Psychology* 27: 333–56.

Mutz, Diana. 1998. *Impersonal Influence: How Perceptions of Mass Collectivities Affect Political Attitudes.* Cambridge: Cambridge University Press.

Nelson, Phillip. 1974. "Advertising as Information." *Journal of Political Economy* 82: 729–54.

O'Gorman, Hubert J. 1979. "White and Black Perceptions of Racial Values." *Public Opinion Quarterly* 43: 48–59.

———. 1986. "The Discovery of Pluralistic Ignorance: An Ironic Lesson." *Journal of the History of the Behavioral Sciences* 22: 333–47.

Okely, Judith. 1986. *Simone de Beauvoir*. New York: Pantheon.

Olson, Mancur. 1971. *The Logic of Collective Action: Public Goods and the Theory of Groups*. Cambridge, Mass.: Harvard University Press.

O'Neill, Barry. 2000. *Honor, Symbols, and War*. Ann Arbor: University of Michigan Press.

Opp, Karl-Dieter, and Christiane Gern. 1993. "Dissident Groups, Personal Networks, and Spontaneous Cooperation: The East German Revolution of 1989." *American Sociological Review* 58: 659–80.

Ottina, Theresa J. 1995. *Advertising Revenues per Television Household: A Market by Market Analysis*. Washington, D.C.: National Association of Broadcasters.

Ozouf, Mona. 1976 [1988]. *Festivals and the French Revolution*. Cambridge, Mass.: Harvard University Press. Translated by Alan Sheridan. Originally published as *La fête revolutionnaire, 1789–1799* (Paris: Gallimard, 1976).

Pastine, Ivan, and Tuvana Pastine. 1999a. "Consumption Externalities, Coordination, and Advertising." Working paper, Bilkent University, Ankara, Turkey.

———. 1999b. "Coordination in Markets with Consumption Externalities: The Role of Advertising and Product Quality." Working paper, Bilkent University, Ankara, Turkey.

Perner, Josef, and Heinz Wimmer. 1985. "'John Thinks That Mary Thinks That . . .' Attribution of Second-Order Beliefs by 5- to 10-Year-Old Children." *Journal of Experimental Child Psychology* 39: 437–71.

Polanyi, Michael. 1958. *Personal Knowledge: Towards a Post-Critical Philosophy*. London: Routledge and Kegan Paul.

Poltrack, David. 1983. *Television Marketing: Network, Local, and Cable*. New York: McGraw-Hill.

Postema, Gerald J. 1982. "Coordination and Convention at the Foundations of Law." *Journal of Legal Studies* 11: 165–203.

Povinelli, Daniel J., and Daniela K. O'Neill. 2000. "Do Chimpanzees Use Their Gestures to Instruct Each Other?" In *Understanding Other Minds: Perspectives from Developmental Cognitive Neuroscience*, edited by Simon Baron-Cohen, Helen Tager-Flusberg, and Donald J. Cohen, pp. 459–87. Oxford: Oxford University Press.

Raboteau, Albert. 1978. *Slave Religion: The "Invisible Institution" of the Antebellum South*. New York: Oxford University Press.

Rapoport, Anatol, and W. J. Horvath. 1961. "A Study of a Large Sociogram." *Behavioral Science* 6: 279–91.

Rattray, R. S. 1923. *Ashanti*. Oxford: Clarendon Press.

Real, Michael R. 1982. "The Super Bowl: Mythic Spectacle." In *Television: The Critical View*, edited by Horace Newcomb, pp. 206–39. Third edition. New York: Oxford University Press.

Reichenbach, Harry. 1931. *Phantom Fame*. New York: Simon and Schuster.

Rendon, Jim. 1998. "Inside the New High-Tech Lock-Downs." *Salon*, September 8. Available at www.salon.com.

Ringle, Ken. 1993. "Debunking the 'Day of Dread' for Women: Data Lacking for Claim of Domestic Violence Surge after Super Bowl." *Washington Post*, January 31, p. A1.

Rothenberg, Randall. 1998. "Bye-Bye." *Wired* 6, no. 1 (January): 72–76.

Rousseau, Jean-Jacques. [1755] 1984. *A Discourse on Inequality*. Translated by Maurice Cranston. Harmondsworth: Penguin Books.

Rubinstein, Ariel. 1989. "The Electronic Mail Game: Strategic Behavior under 'Almost Common Knowledge.'" *American Economic Review* 79: 385–91.

Rutherford, Paul. 1994. *The New Icons? The Art of Television Advertising*. Toronto: University of Toronto Press.

Samuelson, Larry. 1998. *Evolutionary Games and Equilibrium Selection*. Cambridge, Mass.: MIT Press.

Sandburg, Carl. 1936. *The People, Yes*. New York: Harcourt, Brace.

Schelling, Thomas C. 1960 [1980]. *The Strategy of Conflict*. 2d ed. Cambridge, Mass.: Harvard University Press.

Schiffer, Stephen R. 1972. *Meaning*. Oxford: Clarendon Press.

Schor, Juliet B. 1998. *The Overspent American: Upscaling, Downshifting, and the New Consumer*. New York: Basic Books.

Schudson, Michael. 1995. *The Power of News*. Cambridge, Mass.: Harvard University Press.

Schuessler, Alexander A. 2000. *A Logic of Expressive Choice*. Princeton: Princeton University Press.

Schwartz, Tony. 1973. *The Responsive Chord*. New York: Anchor Press.

Scott, James C. 1990. *Domination and the Arts of Resistance: Hidden Transcripts*. New Haven: Yale University Press.

Semple, Janet. 1993. *Bentham's Prison: A Study of the Panopticon Penitentiary*. Oxford: Oxford University Press.

Sen, Amartya K. 1967. "Isolation, Assurance, and the Social Rate of Discount." *Quarterly Journal of Economics* 81: 112–24.

Sewell, William H., Jr. 1985. "Ideologies and Social Revolutions: Reflections on the French Case." *Journal of Modern History* 57: 57–85.

———. 1993. "Toward a Post-Materialist Rhetoric for Labor History." In *Rethinking Labor History*, edited by Lenard R. Berlanstein, pp. 15–38. Urbana: University of Illinois Press.

Shamir, Jacob. 1993. "Pluralistic Ignorance Revisited: Perception of Opinion Distributions in Israel." *International Journal of Public Opinion Research* 5: 22–39.

Shin, Hyun Song. 1996. "Comparing the Robustness of Trading Systems to Higher-Order Uncertainty." *Review of Economic Studies* 63: 39–59.

Signorile, Michelangelo. 1993. *Queer in America: Sex, the Media, and the Closets of Power*. New York: Random House.

———. 1995. *Outing Yourself: How to Come Out as Lesbian or Gay to Your Family, Friends, and Coworkers*. New York: Random House.

Simpson, Glenn R. 1996. "Dole Campaign Has Paid over $1 Million to Firm That Uses Telemarketing to Criticize Opponents." *Wall Street Journal*, March 12, p. A20.

Sivulka, Juliann. 1998. *Soap, Sex, and Cigarettes: A Cultural History of American Advertising*. Belmont, Calif.: Wadsworth.

Sluka, Jeffrey A. 1992. "The Politics of Painting: Political Murals in Northern Ireland." In *The Paths to Domination, Resistance, and Terror*, edited by Carolyn Nordstrom and JoAnn Martin, pp. 18–36. Berkeley: University of California Press.

Sperber, Dan, and Deirdre Wilson. 1986. *Relevance: Communication and Cognition*. Oxford: Basil Blackwell.

Staal, Frits. 1989. *Rules without Meaning: Ritual, Mantras and the Human Sciences*. New York: Peter Lang.

Stellin, Susan. 2000. "Increasingly, E-Mail Users Find They Have Something to Hide." *New York Times*, February 10, p. G8.

Stewart, David W. 1992. "Speculations on the Future of Advertising Research." *Journal of Advertising* 21: 1–18.

Stewart, Ian. 1998. "Mathematical Recreations." *Scientific American* 279, no. 2 (August): 96–97.

"Super TV Ad Jumps into Homes." 1995. *St. Louis Post-Dispatch*, February 1, p. 8C.

Swedberg, Richard. 1990. *Economics and Sociology: Redefining their Boundaries: Conversations with Economists and Sociologists.* Princeton: Princeton University Press.

Tambiah, Stanley Jeyaraja. 1985. "A Performative Approach to Ritual." In *Culture, Thought, and Social Action: An Anthropological Perspective,* pp. 123–66. Cambridge, Mass.: Harvard University Press.

Taylor, Catharine P. 1999. "Netscape's Netcenter and Qwest Communications." *Adweek,* eastern ed., March 8, p. 33.

Tichi, Cecelia. 1991. *Electronic Hearth: Creating an American Television Culture.* New York: Oxford Unviersity Press.

Trow, George W. S. 1997. *Within the Context of No Context.* New York: Atlantic Monthly Press.

Turner, Ralph H., and Lewis M. Killian. 1987. *Collective Behavior.* 3d ed. Englewood Cliffs, N.J.: Prentice-Hall.

Turner, Victor. 1968. *The Drums of Affliction: A Study of Religious Processes among the Ndembu of Zambia.* Oxford: Clarendon Press.

———. 1969. *The Ritual Process: Structure and Anti-Structure.* Ithaca, N.Y.: Cornell University Press.

Turow, Joseph. 1997. *Breaking Up America: Advertisers and the New Media World.* Chicago: University of Chicago Press.

Twitchell, James B. 1996. *Adcult USA: The Triumph of Advertising in American Culture.* New York: Columbia University Press.

Uspensky, B. A. 1975. "'Left' and 'Right' in Icon Painting." *Semiotica* 13: 33–39.

Valente, Thomas W. 1995. *Network Models of the Diffusion of Innovations.* Creskill, N.J.: Hampton Press.

Verba, Sidney. 1965. "The Kennedy Assassination and the Nature of Political Commitment." In *The Kennedy Assassination and the American Public: Social Communication in Crisis,* edited by Bradley S. Greenberg and Edwin B. Parker, pp. 348–60. Stanford: Stanford University Press.

Vinikas, Vincent. 1992. *Soft Soap, Hard Sell: American Hygiene in an Age of Advertisement.* Ames: Iowa State University Press.

Waldmeir, Patti. 1997. *Anatomy of a Miracle: The End of Apartheid and the Birth of the New South Africa.* New York: Norton.

Walters, Ronald G. 1980. "Signs of the Times: Clifford Geertz and Historians." *Social Research* 47: 537–56.

Webster, James G., and Lawrence W. Lichty. 1991. *Ratings Analysis: Theory and Practice.* Hillsdale, N.J.: Lawrence Erlbaum Associates.

Webster, James G., and Patricia F. Phalen. 1997. *The Mass Audience: Rediscovering the Dominant Model.* Mahwah, N.J.: Lawrence Erlbaum Associates.

Weinberger, David. 1995. "The Daily Me? No, the Daily Us." *Wired* 3, no. 4 (April): 108.

Weingast, Barry R. 1997. "The Political Foundations of Democracy and the Rule of Law." *American Political Science Review* 91: 245–63.

Wirth, Michael O., and Harry Bloch. 1985. "The Broadcasters: The Future Role of Local Stations and the Three Networks." In *Video Media Competition: Regulation, Economics, and Technology*, edited by Eli M. Noam, pp. 121–37. New York: Columbia University Press.

Wolcott, James. 1996. "Reborn on the Fourth of July." *New Yorker*, July 15, p. 80–81.

Wolf, Naomi. 1991. *The Beauty Myth: How Images of Beauty Are Used against Women.* New York: Anchor Books.

Wright, Richard. 1945 [1993]. *Black Boy.* New York: HarperPerennial.

Wyatt, Justin. 1994. *High Concept: Movies and Marketing in Hollywood.* Austin: University of Texas Press.

Young, Peyton. 1996. "The Economics of Convention." *Journal of Economic Perspectives* 10: 105–22.

———. 1998. *Individual Strategy and Social Structure: An Evolutionary Theory of Institutions.* Princeton: Princeton University Press.

Zoglin, Richard. 1993. "When the Revolution Comes, What Will Happen To . . ." *Time*, April 12, p. 56.

Index